An Italian American Story

A Memoir
by
Susan D'Angelo Mannino

Cover Design by Elizabeth Uhlig

MARBLE HOUSE EDITIONS

Published by Marble House Editions

96-09 66th Avenue (Suite 1D)

Rego Park, NY 11374

Library of Congress Cataloguing-in-Publication Data

Mannino, Susan D'Angelo

An Italian American Story/by Susan D'Angelo Mannino

Summary: The chronicle and memoir of an Italian American family living in Queens during the second half of the 20th century.

ISBN: 978-0-9815345-3-4

Library of Congress Catalog Card Number 2008935414

Printed in China

In loving memory of my father, Giovan Battista D'Angelo,
and in celebration of everyone in our family.

Susan D'Angelo Mannino

Introduction

July 9, 2006 - Viva l'Italia

Italy beats France 5-3 for the World Cup in soccer. What a day to be an Italian American.

Nothing makes Italian people crazier than World Cup soccer. The World Cup is to Italians what the World Series is to New York Mets and Yankees fans. The Subway Series. Only in baseball the Mets and Yankees have a shot at winning every year. In soccer, Italy and all the other countries have only one chance in four years to win the World Cup. This victory for Italy was number four. The only team with more victories is Brazil, with five wins.

I watched the game in 1994 when Italy lost to Brazil by penalty shots after a 0-0 draw. The anguish on Roberto Biaggio's face was enough to break my heart. I just wanted to hug the guy. In a show of loyalty to Italy and the Azzuri, proud Italians were out everywhere with their Italian flags and T-shirts, despite the team's having lost. My cousin even put a red, white, and green ribbon on her Shitzu. People were stopping us as we drove around so they could take pictures and videotape the dog.

My husband, my son, and I were watching the 2006 final game at home on Channel 7. Our neighbors called while the score was still 1-0, France's favor. They invited us over for a barbecue, but my neighbor knew we would not go anywhere unless we could watch the game. Nice guy that he is, he hooked up a television set in the backyard. Unless there is an emergency, don't even think of calling an Italian American household while Italy is playing for the World

1

Cup, because one of two things may happen: either they will hang up on you or they will not answer the telephone at all. But if you are lucky, they may just invite you over to watch the game with them.

Even our neighbors, Juan and Yolanda, were rooting for Italy. We warned our friends in advance that whether or not Italy won, we were ready to hit the streets in our car, my son in his *Italia* baseball cap, I with the Italian flag. My husband would be driving and honking the horn. They understood. So as we ate our food in front of the set, our friends were cheering with us.

My husband and I were riveted to the set, praying silently as the two teams played a brutal game. The captain of the French team, Zinedine Zidane, gave a mean head butt to Italian player Marco Materazzi. *What a way to be remembered*, I thought, for Zidane was set to retire after this game.

The score was 1-1 and went into overtime, and even after overtime it was still a draw.

Then came the penalty shots. I put my son's cap on my head and held it as I prayed. As Fabio Grosso made that last shot, my husband and I flew out of our seats. I jumped right on him and he almost fell. We ran over to grab our son and passed him around like a football. We covered his face with kisses. The Azzuri players danced the *Tarantella* right there on the field. I wanted to jump through the screen and dance with them.

We Italian Americans take our heritage very seriously. Nothing brings us closer as *paesani* than World Cup Soccer. We grabbed our son and headed for our car. Just as we planned, our son was in the back seat wearing his *Italia* cap. I was in the passenger seat with the Italian flag out the window. The first place we headed to was Fresh Pond Road in Ridgewood, Queens, where I had grown up. The cars were bumper to bumper, everyone honking horns and waving flags and screaming out their windows. Italy had not won the World Cup since 1982. Everyone on Fresh Pond Road was Italian that day. Even an Asian man was waving his arms and shouting, "Italia!"

One man made me laugh and cry at the same time. He lifted his blue *Forza Italia* T-shirt and pounded his fist on his belly. He chanted, "I-talia, I-talia, I-talia!" Then he ran up to car windows to hug and kiss people on both cheeks. It was beautiful. I still don't know if he actually knew the people he was kissing, but they did not seem to mind.

After cruising around the old neighborhood, we headed home. The teenagers, some of them third or fourth generation in The United States, would be out until dawn celebrating Italy's victory. I told my son to look around and pay attention. "Look, baby. Look at all of these people. They are Italian Americans, just like you. Your *nonnos* and *nonnas* were born in Italy, just like mine. Be proud to be Italian American. Be very proud!"

Then my son, just four and a half years old, started chanting from the back seat, "I-talia, I- talia, I-talia!" That is the thing about my generation. We are glad to be in America but never compromise our loyalty to be being Italian. Especially when it comes to soccer.

Italy could not have picked a better time to win. I was almost a year into my writing when the Azzuri won the World Cup in the summer of 2006. What better way to illustrate Italian American pride than the World Cup and all the chaos that followed? *Grazie, Italia!*

This is my story, the story of my family. I want to take you on a journey back to the 1940s and introduce you to my grandparents. I will continue into the 1950s as my parents marry and start their own family. Then we'll stroll down Memory Lane during the 1970s and 1980s when I was a kid, and then a teenager.

In the summer of 1990 something happened in our family that would change all of us forever. I will tell you all about that last year, how life was just before it happened. I hope you enjoy reading about my family. The ups, the downs, and in betweens. I hope you enjoy our story. *An Italian American Story.*

Part One

Northern Africa, 1943 - How It All Started

It was during World War II when two strangers met in a military hospital. The first man, Orazio, had suffered a stroke when he was told his wife and three daughters had been killed in a plane crash. The second man, Bernardo, was suffering from an unremembered ailment.

Both men were Italian. Orazio came from a Sicilian town named Modica, and Bernardo from Castellamare del Golfo, Sicily, although he had been born in Rome. As they shared a hospital room and told their stories to each other, the two men formed a strong, lifelong bond that neither of them could have possibly expected.

This was Orazio's story: an Italian soldier stationed in Tripoli, he was married to Giuseppa, a Sicilian girl from the town of Gella. They had four daughters and one son, and when Orazio had last seen his wife, she was eight months pregnant.

Orazio and Giuseppa's first child, Maria, had already grown up to be a beautiful young woman. It was rumored that the foreign soldiers had been taking advantage of young, innocent women, and so Orazio ordered Giuseppa to take Maria and their two youngest daughters, Carmela and Silvana, out of Tripoli and back to safety in Italy. His two older children, Rocco and Rosaria, were already at a *colonia*, a kind of camp for adolescent boys and girls that served as a boarding school, in Northern Italy. It was a safe holding area for these children during wartime.

Orazio was told by a military officer that Giuseppa and their three daughters had all been killed in a plane crash on their way back to Sicily. "Word has come," he said, "that there were no survivors." This horrible shock brought on Orazio's stroke and would ultimately end his life at the young age of forty.

Bernardo's story was different: once a sailor in Castellamare, he was now stationed in Libya as part of a rescue team for the Italian army. When there were bombings, the rescuers would search the land for the injured, dying and dead.

Bernardo's wife Maria was a native of Castellamare del Golfo. She and Bernardo had five children at the time: Francesca, Battista, Margherita, Giuseppina, and Benedetto. Later they had another child, whom they named Maria. The first son was named for his paternal grandfather, Giovan Battista, and was called Battista for short.

It was Bernardo who would someday share the story of how he and Orazio met. He would tell of their brief but meaningful stay in the hospital. Two Italian men shared a piece of their lives in a North African hospital. These two men were my grandfathers.

Orazio's wife and daughters did not, in fact, perish on that plane. There was a crash and a small fire, but the fire had been contained. Orazio died during the war, believing his pregnant wife and his daughters died because of his insistence on their returning to Sicily. Although Giuseppa and her three daughters survived, Giuseppa's unborn baby did not. Shortly after Giuseppa arrived in Sicily, the baby was taken from her during an emergency delivery. Giuseppa and Orazio's baby boy was stillborn as a result of the trauma.

Giuseppa took several months to recover from the emergency procedure that took her dead infant from her womb. During the first few months she was not even able to walk and was on bed rest at her mother's home in Sicily. Once she recovered, though, she set out to Northern Italy alone to search for her other children. She had since lost contact with Rocco and Rosaria and had left Carmela and Silvana in the care of her mother and sister Margherita.

A year went by and Giuseppa returned with only Rosaria. She also brought back with her a niece and the daughter of a family friend. She cared for these young girls until she was able to contact their families to come and take them home. Rocco would eventually find his way back to Sicily on his own.

During the war and in its aftermath in the mid-forties, work was scarce in Sicily, and there was an extensive migration of Italian citizens to Tripoli and Tunisia. Maria, Rosaria, and Rocco, young adults by then, had married in Sicily. Rosaria and her husband, part of this migration, went to live in Tripoli. Giuseppa's parents, Salvatore and Sara, had also migrated to North Africa.

Giuseppa had lost all contact with Orazio after he ordered her back to Sicily. All the years in between she had no idea if her husband was dead or alive, and so she was forced to raise her five children alone. In 1946, a year after the war ended, Giuseppa, while still in Sicily, received word from the Red Cross that Orazio had died on September 3, 1943. The cause of his death was never really revealed. Some said it was a stroke brought on by the shock of his perceived loss. Sometimes it was explained as a "broken heart." So young herself, Giuseppa never remarried.

In June of 1948, Giuseppa followed her parents back to Tripoli and moved in with them. Rocco came later on with his wife and their first son, Vincenzo. Maria joined them as well with her daughters.

In time, the widowed Giuseppa and her parents, Salvatore and Sara, came to live next door to Bernardo and Maria. Giuseppa and Orazio's little daughter fell in love with Bernardo and Maria's first son, Giovan Battista. They were married in 1956.

Silvana and Battista are my parents. I have asked my mother if she has any recollection of her father. She doesn't, but she does remember the photograph in which the whole family is in mourning. My mother was only a small child, but in that photograph even she was dressed in black. Could my grandmother

Giuseppa have ever guessed that these two families would become linked by such a series of coincidences?

I often wonder if Nonno Orazio had something to do with my parents' destiny. Perhaps up there from heaven, he brought Silvana and Battista together. I can't be sure, but I am thankful they met.

* * *

The Present Day - New York City

My parents got married when my mother was sixteen and my father twenty-three. They had six children together but their second daughter died when she was eleven days old. So we are five siblings, four girls and one boy, and I am the youngest.

My brother and sisters are named according to old Sicilian tradition, where every baby's name is chosen in honor of a grandparent or a close relative. The first male child especially is named for the paternal grandfather in order to carry on the family name. My brother Bernardo is named for our paternal grandfather; Maria for our paternal grandmother. Josephine is named for our maternal grandmother, and Francesca for our father's eldest sister. Then I came along — Susan, the American. I am the only child born in America, and so my parents insisted upon an American name. When Italian people ask me, "*Come ti chiami?*" I reply, "Susanna." Close enough.

I was just a baby as my siblings were growing up. As I got older I heard the stories about how life had been for the children before me. Apparently my life with Dad was easy compared to Maria's - she could not breathe without permission. And Josephine was always in trouble. Bernardo was supposed to be the perfect son, but by his own admission, he never could figure out what that meant. He really just wanted to be a kid. Francesca was as close to perfect as she tried to be. She was always buried in her schoolwork, vowing to herself that with a good education she would not be poor. Francesca actually studied the dictionary. She looked up new words every morning to improve and enrich her vocabulary.

Francesca inherited Dad's beautifully structured face. We all have the eyes. Even I, the only one who looks just like my mother, I have the same eyes. *L'occhi di Chrasto* is how Dad's cousin once described them to me. She said in his earlier years Dad could look at anyone with those big, deep eyes and stop them in their tracks. For us, Dad's eyes were, in a sense, his voice. The moment you asked for something or to go somewhere, you had your answer. No words necessary.

I never understood how much my father loved me until I had my own child. I always resented the early curfews, the hundreds of questions, the millions of lectures. I could not understand why he would spend hours looking out our window as I played outside on a Sunday afternoon. I could not go to a friend's house unless he had the telephone number. I could not go to a school dance unless my cousins or friends came over and begged him to let me go. And if I did get to go, they had to pick me up and walk me home right afterward. There he was, looking out that window until I reached the front steps.

I thought then that Dad did not trust me. Now that I am a mother I understand. It is funny how sometimes I speak to my son and flinch. As the words leave my mouth, I recall moments in my life when I was the kid and heard the same words from my father's mouth.

It has been a long time since my father died. Now I would give anything for an interrogation or a lecture. When I pass through the old neighborhood, I drive down our block and look up at that window, trying so hard to see his face. I miss his face. I miss his voice. I miss my father. They say time heals all wounds. I disagree. The older I get, the more I feel my father's absence. I missed Dad at my wedding. I cried out, "Daddy, help me!" as I gave birth to my son. I miss him every day of my life.

So many memories are safe with me. My father was the anchor of our family. We feared him, respected him, and loved him. He was the heart in all of us. The older we grew, the more he loved us. He would joke about the lottery sometimes. "If I win, I buy a big house so I could live there with my kids and their families." Only he never played. Instead he spent any extra money he had on music cassettes and later on video cassettes. He loved his Italian music and his westerns. He made *me* fall in love with musicals. *An American in Paris. The Sound of Music.* He would rent them on the weekend and we would watch them over and over again. Sometimes we would catch a movie marathon on PBS. We stayed up many nights watching Danny Kaye or Fred and Ginger. Like all children, or most, I thought he would always be there. I was so mistaken.

* * *

Summer, 1989

It is amazing how quickly life changes. The summer of 1989 is what I now refer to as "The Beginning of the End." That June, my cousin Stephanie was getting married in Florida. Mom and I had planned on going to the wedding from the moment we heard about the engagement. Mom's sister, Zia Carmela, would come with us, as well as Zia Adriana and Zio Filippo, my parents' best friends. We rented a modest condo for the week and were going to make a vacation out of it. Dad wanted to come too, but had no vacation time left at work.

One day, when Mom had been out all afternoon with Zia Carmela and Zia Adriana, they decided to pick up Dad from his job at the hospital before going home. When they arrived there, they found Dad waiting with a big grin on his face. They expected to hear some kind of news, but there Dad sat, grinning.

The women wondered what Dad was up to. "I have a nice surprise," he told them. "I got too jealous that you were all going to Florida without me. I am going to come with you."

The women looked at each other then at him. "You sure?" Mom questioned. "I remember you said you have no vacation time left at work."

Dad explained that his supervisor had heard him lamenting to friends during lunch. He had said that he felt bad because he could not make it to Stephanie's wedding and that he could not spend a week on vacation with Mom and me. "John, isn't that your baby?" his supervisor asked.

"Yes, she is almost nineteen years old but she is still my baby," Dad answered.

The supervisor took Dad's hand and led him to her office. "Let me see here what we can do." She went to a metal file cabinet and took out a manila file folder with Dad's name on it. She flipped through several pages, jotting down numbers on a legal pad. Then with a smile on her face she looked up and turned to Daddy. "Okay, Mr. John, you are all set to go. You have some sick days, some personal days, and you have a couple of floating holidays. Enjoy your family!"

Dad threw his hands in the air. He grabbed his supervisor's face and kissed her on both cheeks. As her cheeks turned red, Dad teased, "My wife cannot get mad at me because I can go now on vacation!" Mom sucked her teeth when Dad told that part. Then she gave him a dirty look. The other women looked at the two of them and then everyone began to laugh. "I cannot wait to tell Susie," Dad said.

Mom and Dad's two *commares* were thrilled that Dad would be joining us. He was close with both my aunts. Zia Adriana is married to Dad's best friend Filippo, and she is also Mom's best friend. Our two families were always together. Every summer we went on picnics together and during the year we shared holidays. Because Mom and Dad didn't drive, we all traveled together. Imagine four adults and nine kids in a big blue station wagon. As the older daughters got boyfriends, there were more cars to get around in.

Dad's brother and sisters were all living back in Italy, so friends were especially valuable to him. He loved and respected these friends as if they were his own siblings. Their children called him

Zio and they loved him. He loved them right back.

Zia Carmela, Mom's older sister, was really like a sister to Dad. In Tripoli, she ran with the same crowd that Dad did. They were at the same parties and the same dances at the local church. Zia Carmela had been through a personal tragedy early in her life. She was married to Zio Raffaele, who was Dad's best friend at that time. Dad and Raffaele were working at the same construction site when they met. Daddy was an ironworker and Raffaele did the accounting for the company.

About six months into their marriage, Zio Raffaele died. Carmela was devastated, and was also two months pregnant. She would later give birth to a baby girl whom she named Raffaela. In hopes of giving her daughter a better life, Carmela set out for what she heard was "the land of opportunity." A woman alone and unfamiliar with the English language, Zia Carmela took her baby and a suitcase and immigrated to The United States of America.

Upon arriving in the U.S., Carmela lived with her sister Maria, who was already in America with her husband Achille, and their children. She worked in a factory and saved enough money to rent her own apartment. She sent for Nonna Giuseppa, and in May of 1964, Nonna Giuseppa came to America to help her widowed daughter. Nonna cared for Raffaela while Zia Carmela went to work to feed and clothe her daughter.

When my parents came to America, five months after Nonna Giuseppa did, they also lived in Zia Carmela's house. They stayed with Zia until they both found jobs and could rent their own apartment. They were four adults and five children living in a four-room apartment.

One year after Carmela arrived in America, she married Zio Angelo, who was her first cousin. Zio Angelo had admired Carmela since they were barely teenagers. He wrote a letter to Nonna Giuseppa expressing his desire to wed Carmela. He came to the States from Northern Italy, where he then lived, and he and Carmela were married. They had two sons together, Rocco and Salvatore.

After a shared childhood and the loss of Zio Raffaele, Dad and Carmela remained close through the ensuing years. Dad was like a friend and brother to Zia Carmela. He was someone she could always talk to, confide in.

On the day that my father got permission to go to Florida, I came home from work to find my parents conspiring in the kitchen. After raising five children together they had developed a secret language. I just knew something was up when my father called, "Come here Sweetheart, *ti voglio parlare!*" which meant he had something *important* to tell me.

This time I was not in trouble. Dad announced to me that he was coming to Florida with Mom and me. I nearly knocked him over with my embrace. This would be the second time I traveled with both of my parents. I barely remembered the time before that because I was only about five years old.

That time, Nonno Bernardo was very ill. Mom, Dad, and I flew Alitalia to Palermo. We went straight to the hospital from the airport. Before the trip, my father had taught me how to say, "Nonno, I love you very much," in Italian.

We were brought to the floor Nonno Bernardo was on. We had no idea what he was ailing from and he had no idea we were coming to see him, so the mood was a bit tense. I was nudged into a large, sterile room. It smelled of alcohol and was devoid of any warmth – no pictures, no hint of softness. A charmless room to which the patient had to bring his own sheets.

My parents left the door just an inch or two ajar so they could listen. I ran to the bedside of this elderly man with only strands of white hair on his head. He had tired eyes and a chubby face. As he turned and looked at me I recited perfectly, *"Nonno, ti voglio tanto bene!"* (Those were the only Italian words I knew, except for *Mamma* and *Papà*.)

The old man began to weep. *"Sango mio,"* he cried, *"Mia nipote."* My blood. My grandchild. Nonno Bernardo recognized me from photographs, and probably recognized my mother's childhood face in mine. He knew I had to be Silvana's baby.

During the next three weeks, we went on a continuous tour of relatives' homes. There was a steady stream of conversation, questions, and food. We visited Castellamare, where my father was born, and enjoyed the tremendous fuss that our huge family made over us, the *Americans*.

I remember very little of Italy, and what I do remember seems like a daydream to me now, one that resides in the senses, particularly those related to food. I remember how good the butter smelled when, at lunch and dinner, I devoured *pasta con burro*. Or the way the ice cream tasted and felt in the mouth. It looked like vanilla but had little bits of nuts in it. Now, as a grown up, I know it's called *nucciola*.

Mom tells me all I wanted for breakfast was cereal, which of course, is not an Italian custom. An American child simply does not want pastries and sweet black coffee for breakfast. No, my parents had to run around Palermo to find the kind of cereal I wanted: Captain Crunch.

When we returned to America, I had had to learn how to speak English again but Italian never left me, and the few memories of Italy stuck with me as well. Perhaps this is because Mom and Dad would talk about that trip all the time. They constantly reminisced about the reuniting of the family, how I, a small child, had picked up the language so fast, and they relived the avalanche of attention that everyone had showered upon me.

On the trip to Florida I was two months short of turning nineteen, and the airplane ticket was a birthday gift from my parents. It was pure happiness for me to be with both of my parents. It took two flights to reach Daytona Beach. The first leg of the journey was out of Kennedy into Raleigh, North Carolina, with a one-hour layover.

My father and Zio Filippo looked so handsome in their pressed slacks and cotton shirts. Years past middle age, they cleverly hid bald spots with what remained of their graying hair. They were clean shaven and fresh smelling.

My father paced around the airport, his hands going in and out of his pockets and his eyes wandering all around. Those damn *No Smoking* signs. But somehow he found a quiet little corner and summoned my uncle and me to stand guard. He pulled out a pack of cigarettes from his shirt pocket and lit one up. *So many trips to the store as a little girl. That soft red foil package with the thick white stripe in the center and big black lettering.*

As a child, I found my father's habit annoying. In my teenage years, his habit became a convenience for me because I would always see friends on the way to the store and take an hour to get back. I would complain about how crowded the store was and how long I had to wait in line for his "stupid cigarettes." But with one glance at his eyes, I knew it was time to shut up. *Quit while you're ahead!* they warned me.

After Dad had his cigarette, it was time to board our next flight. My parents sat together, and Zio Filippo and Zia Adriana sat in front of them. Zia Carmela and I were behind them. As the flight attendant went through the safety precautions, I silently mocked her with my hands. This made Zia Carmela laugh. Dad looked back at us. I was reminded of a joke his godchild Concetta told me.

Concetta is Zio Filippo's eldest daughter. A year earlier, when I graduated High School, I spent a month in Florida with Zio, Zia and Concetta. It was a blast. One night Concetta and I had a little too much *vino*. Connie had me stand beside her and demonstrate a flight attendant giving emergency directions. As I did so, I got to the part where you assume crash position and put your head between your legs. Connie did as I did then kissed her hand and slapped her own butt. I said to Daddy, *"Okay, Papà, ora bacia cullo, ed arriverderci!"*

Zia Carmela laughed out loud. Daddy's face was beet red as he too laughed. "Shhh!!!" Mom scolded, but she had no idea what we were laughing at.

Daddy winked at me. "You're just as bad as your father," he said.

Upon arrival at the condo, we dropped our things and went grocery shopping at a local supermarket. God forbid visitors should come and there was no food to offer them! Soon there were relatives everywhere. You could smell the aroma of garlic and olive oil emanating from the small kitchen and flowing through the whole condo. Everyone was eating all around the place, wherever they could find a spot to sit or stand. Grated cheese was being passed around from one hand to another. Mom was going around the room filling any kind of available glass with wine. The kids tried to sneak their glasses but my mother was sharp. *"No, no per te, c'è la soda in cucina."*

The kids my age just sneaked a bottle outside by the pool with some plastic cups and had our own party. We sat there catching up on family gossip. Then we heard music blaring from a distance, *Era li che voleva volare, l'uccelino della commare.* We all finished the verse then started laughing. Someone yelled out, "New York is in the house!"

We did a lot of visiting that week. So much of our extended family had moved to Florida in the '80s. We had all started out in Brooklyn together. Then we moved to Queens. Some of the cousins moved to other states. By the late '80s most of the family had settled in Florida. Life in New York can be very difficult and very expensive. The winters here can be brutally cold. The summers can get incredibly muggy. Then, in my opinion, the rents and prices of homes are obscene. It's just like the famous lyrics, *"…if you can make it there, you'll make it anywhere…"* I suppose my relatives figured since they had survived life in New York they could make a life for themselves anywhere. Besides, warm weather and palm trees can be very alluring.

My mother's older sister, my Zia Rosaria, and her husband Zio Rocco, were the first to make the move with their two youngest children. Even though Mom and Rosaria are grandmothers, Zia Rosaria still treats Mom like a baby. This relationship was forged when they were young and has never changed.

Zia Rosaria enlightened Mom about pregnancy and childbirth. When Mom and Dad first eloped, they had no place to live, so they stayed with Rosaria and Rocco. (To confuse the story, Rosaria and Mom also had a brother named Rocco.) One day while their husbands were at work, Rosaria approached her newlywed sister. "What's wrong Silvana?" Rosaria asked.

"I don't feel too good," explained Silvana. "I just feel tired and my stomach is upside down. Now I have a headache too. I'm just a little sick but I will be fine," she conceded.

Rosaria could not help but laugh at her sister's innocence. "You are not sick Silvana, you must be pregnant."

Silvana got up from her chair, startled by her sister's remark. "Are you crazy, Rosaria, *sei patsa!* I just got married. Let me get settled first. Not a baby now!"

Rosaria motioned for her sister to sit down beside her again. "Do you sleep with your husband, Silva, or not?"

Instead of a verbal, "Of course I do!" Mom just gave her a childish smirk. Rosaria held her sister's hands in her own. As gently as possible, she explained what Mom should expect if she was pregnant. Then she went on to explain childbirth as well. Mom had assumed that a doctor would always cut open a woman's belly, remove the baby and then stitch the woman back up. Of course, the woman would be knocked out with drugs. She had no idea about natural childbirth.

As Rosaria explained, Mom's face was turning green and her eyes were opened wide. Suddenly she had had enough. She sprang up from her seat and yelled at her sister, "Rosaria shut up! You are teasing me. You are trying to scare me. How could a baby come out of *there*. It's *impossible!*"

Silvana was crying as she ran to another room to throw up the rest of her lunch. Rosaria followed her, and as Silvana heaved, Rosaria just smiled in silence. She gently held back Silvana's hair, thinking to herself that her baby sister was about to grow up whether she was ready to or not.

Zia Rosaria went on to be an expert on childbirth. Of all the sisters, she had the greatest number of children. Rosaria had her first child, also named Connie, when she was sixteen. She and Zio Rocco had four daughters and three sons at first. In the late '60s, Mom and Dad decided they would have another child, one born in America. They had been trying to conceive for more than a year when Zia Rosaria got a surprise. And a few weeks after Zia found out she was pregnant, Mom realized she was, too. Nine months later, Zia had a baby girl, her eighth child, whom she named Stephanie.

My cousin Stephanie and I came along in the summer of 1970. We are the youngest of Orazio and Giuseppa's twenty-five grandchildren. In fact, I am the youngest of us all. In the 8mm films of the '70s you will see all the older kids passing Stephanie and me around like little dolls. Some of the older cousins have children who are older than Stephanie and me. It is cool actually, being the youngest of all those cousins. No matter how many years go by or how old I get, I am always treated like a baby doll. It doesn't help matters that I still have chubby cheeks. My cousins still cannot resist squeezing and kissing my face when they see me.

Memories come flooding in when I see family and I get that affection from them. I think back now how as a kid, I loved to sleep at Zia Rosaria's house. Stephanie and I would stay up late playing and laughing. Zia Rosaria would make us a special breakfast in the morning, toast with melted butter and soft boiled eggs cracked open and poured into a bowl. We would dip the toast to soak up the warm egg and use a spoon and our fingers to eat the last drops.

Zia Rosaria let us drink *latte e caffè*, espresso with hot milk and lots of sugar. Once we finished our breakfast, Zia Rosaria brushed our hair and styled it the same way, usually in pigtails or ponytails. Then she would give us each a hug, a kiss on the cheek, and slap us on our bottoms. "Okay, my *sale e peppe*, go play now." Salt and pepper. Stephanie is blonde with light eyes and pale skin. I am a brunette with dark eyes and olive skin. These were Zia Rosaria's nicknames for us, her *Sale e Peppe*. (Who knew years later there would be a rap duo named *Salt-n-Pepa*?)

I was rarely allowed to sleep at anyone's house. Daddy would warn me before going out. *"Non mi chiedere, per dormire li va bene!"* Don't ask me to let you sleep there. But I never listened. Stephanie would put on her Shirley Temple smile as soon as we arrived. Stephanie would go to Daddy's side. I would go over to Mom. Then as Stephanie batted her pretty eyes she pleaded, "Zio Battista, could Susie pleeeeeease sleep over tonight?" Dad would look at me with the *eyes*.

I would shrug my shoulders. "I didn't ask," I'd say. "Stephanie did." That was my defense.

Dad looked at Stephanie and said, *"Vediamo*, we will see."

Stephanie and I had a backup plan. We were ready in case that *"Vediamo"* turned into a "No!" We would walk away feigning defeat with frowning faces that only cute little girls could pull off. As soon as we got to Stephanie's room, the frowns would disappear. We would read our books and dress up in Stephanie's dresses, pretending to be royalty. Then we would just be silly and have fun, the way little kids do best.

Eventually we heard the grownups getting ready to leave. As the chairs were pulled away from the tables and the loud voices were saying, *"Okay, ci vediamo,"* we would resort to Plan B. Stephanie and I would drop our toys and jump on the bed. A miracle — we were asleep in seconds! Zia Rosaria and Mom would come in to get me. Our accomplices. *"Guarda gia stanno dormire."* Look, they are already asleep.

I can just imagine how Zia Rosaria and Mom must have looked at one another and smiled. Then they would come over and kiss us on the cheek. One of them would tease us. "Okay, my little monkeys, stay in bed and be quiet." They would go into the other room and Zia Rosaria would tell Daddy, *"Battista, la bambina sta dormire. Lascia Susie per stasera,"* urging him to let the "baby" sleep. Daddy must have smiled too. We would hear him walk into Stephanie's room and could feel him looking at us asleep on the bed. Then he would come over and kiss us each on the forehead.

"Goodnight" he'd say. "You two are full of bologna." Stephanie and I could not help but laugh. *"Buona notte,"* he'd whisper again.

"Good night Daddy!" I called out. "I love you." Dad would look back at me and wrinkle his nose and wink.

"Good night, Sweetheart. I love you too." Then he'd turn off the light on his way out of the room. As soon as we heard the front door close, Stephanie and I would jump out of bed. Zia Rosaria would let us play until she finished cleaning up the dining room.

I was so sad when Stephanie moved to Florida with her parents and her brother Robbie. We were both about twelve years old then. When Zia Rosaria and Zio Rocco moved, their married children followed them. The only one left in New York now is my cousin Tony.

Down in Florida on our family trip, we had many relatives to visit. Zia Adriana also took us to visit some of the model homes in the adjoining communities. Zia Rosaria was trying to twist Daddy's arm into moving to Florida and it was starting to work. Daddy loved the ocean. So did Mom. As we admired the new homes, the three of us daydreamed.

"When I retire, Silva, we could move here. We will get a nice little house on the beach and *ci passiamo la vecchiaia.*"

I pouted. *"La vecchiaia...*in your old age I'm coming with you. You

19

are not leaving me!"

Mom and Dad laughed at me. All the while the three of us hoped the whole family would follow us as Zia Rosaria's kids had. "The boys would love it here," Mom reflected.

Dad looked at the pool in the backyard. "Someday," he said pensively. "Someday."

That Saturday was Stephanie's wedding. It was a beautiful sunny day. All of us were all bronzed from a week at the pool and beach. It had not sunk in for me yet that my Stephanie was getting married. She even brought me to her final fitting the first day we arrived in Florida. Seeing her in that white lace gown and jeweled headpiece should have made it real for me, but somehow it didn't. I just remembered us as little girls playing dress up. Stephanie looked like one of the princesses we read about in our storybooks. Those golden ringlets and pretty eyes.

Stephanie would use her age against me sometimes, like when we were arguing. "You should respect your elders!" she would yell at me. The truth is we are only eleven days apart. All I could think of was Zia Rosaria's *Salt and Pepper*. Thank God for waterproof mascara!

I sat with the young, single people at the reception and my parents sat with the other aunts and uncles. As always with family weddings, there was dancing all night. Daddy could be found among the young people. He was either twirling me or one of my cousins around. When he got tired, he'd go have a drink.

As Stephanie and her father danced together, the D.J. played the old song *Daddy's Little Girl*. Daddy found his way through the crowd to be beside me as we watched Stephanie and Zio. He put an arm around me and I leaned my head back on his shoulder. I put my hand over his.

"When it is your turn, we use this song too. You are my little girl." I just nodded, unable to speak as those eyes of his shone back at me.

This time it was I who was thinking *Someday, someday.*

Our last day at the condo fell on Father's Day, a crystal clear Sunday morning. We spent the early part of our day by the pool. We lazed around in blue and white striped lounge chairs, no doubt recovering from the night before. After lunch we walked along the shore and took in the view. The sun was a radiant gold, the ocean a sapphire blue. The only sounds were the waves hitting the sand and children laughing as they built and destroyed sandcastles. A flock of birds was flying back and forth across the sky above our heads. Paradise.

I was strolling with my father and Zio Filippo, our arms linked. The others were right behind us. Suddenly Dad took off his slippers, immune to the heat of the sand beneath his feet. The Florida sun was brutal that day. His brown face was drenched. Then he challenged himself. "Let me see if I am an old man yet!" he said. He wiped the sweat off his face with the back of his arm and charged into the water. I froze where I stood.

"What's he doing?" I cried.

"It's OK", Mom said. "He has been swimming since he was a little boy."

***

As a young girl, I stayed up nights with my father as he shared with me tales of his childhood. Daddy was born in the fishing town of Castellamare del Golfo, Sicily. He was only about seven or eight years old when he ran through the streets at dawn summoning the fisherman to their duties. His formal academics ended by the third grade, and his real teachers were the men who allowed him to tag along on their boats. They taught him about the land, the sea, and the stars.

When I was growing up, we had a clothesline outside our kitchen window. Some nights, Mom would ask Dad, *"Battista posso lasciare la robba? Pensi che deve piovere?"* to see if it were safe to hang out the clothes or if he foresaw rain. Dad would walk to the window and look up at the stars and the sky. At times, without even bothering Mom, he would just open up the window and take the clothes in and leave them laid out on the kitchen table. Mom would find them when she came into the kitchen and proceed to place the damp clothing on chairs and radiators to dry inside the apartment. Wouldn't you know it, the next morning we would wake to rain.

In the 1930s, when Nonno Bernardo went to Tripoli with the Italian Army, he brought along his wife, children, and his father, Giovan Battista. Then in 1940 when Mussolini declared war on Great Britain, the English came into Libya across the Tunisian border. At that time Nonno Bernardo and the others in his division received these orders from their superiors: "Due to recent activity, we are making aircraft available to return your families to Sicily. We feel the women and children will be safer there. This transport will take place immediately." Nonna Maria, along with her father-in-law, took the children back to Castellamare del Golfo.

Although Daddy was seven years old at the time, he became the man of the house in his father's absence. His grandfather, Giovan Battista, went to live with his daughters upon his return to Sicily but he always stayed close to Bernardo's family.

Daddy worked on the boats and learned all he could from the men who became his mentors. They looked at this young boy and admired his courage. He had no fear. Merely a child, he believed he was a man already. One day one of the men was teasing Daddy about his fearlessness. "You believe you are invincible," he said, "but let's see how brave you really are." Daddy, a child with a cigarette hanging from his lips, turned to this man with "the eyes." The man turned his face so as to not laugh at him directly.

Then he thought a moment and said, "Okay, if you *are* brave, you see the length of this pier? There is a hole the size of a tire on one end, and another hole the same size at the other end of it. If you have all this courage and believe that you are a man of the sea, let's see if you can swim beneath this pier from one end to the other."

Daddy pulled the cigarette from his mouth and stepped on it with his sandaled foot. He smiled at the man, nodded his head, and jumped into the water. He found exactly that spot with an opening to the inside of the pier, just the size of a bicycle tire, and swam through it. He swam under that pier with the anticipation of making a fool out of that all-too-pompous man who would be waiting for him to fail, or perhaps not even reappear. Suddenly he saw a light at the other end. *I could not stay still on my seat as Daddy would tell me this part, feeling the anxiety as if I were there with him.* He would reappear with a splash back into the water to find that man and his companions waiting for this boy to show up.

Well, that same man almost choked on his own cigarette, which fell right out of his mouth with the shock of seeing Daddy in the water. The men who were there, including the large, tough one who initiated the dare, began to applaud for Daddy. The young Battista jumped up on that pier and just nodded his head as he passed that man, smiling as he walked by.

That'll show him, Daddy thought to himself. That's how he used to tell it to me. Then he'd laugh as he'd playfully slap my hand and shake it, amused as he saw the look of amazement on my innocent face.

Daddy and the others in the family earned their living in different ways. They had to because they did not know if Nonno Bernardo would ever return. For eight years they had no way of knowing whether he was still alive or if he had been killed during the war.

Nonno Bernardo also had no word of his family for many years. During that time Nonna Maria was on her own in Castellamare. She was a proud woman and refused to give the townspeople a chance to say anything about her or her children. She insisted they be well-mannered and well groomed. They always had freshly pressed clothing and neatly combed hair. Despite the need for Nonna Maria to hold many jobs, her home, in which she raised her five children alone, was always spotless. She loved plants, and her house and front yard were filled with greenery. Unable to purchase fertilizer, she would instruct her children to collect fresh manure when they saw one of the animals relieve itself. Her children did whatever their mother instructed and were always ready to help her showcase her many talents, including her gardening skills.

Nonna Maria worked at a sardine factory cleaning and packaging fish to prepare it for sale. She and her children also worked, *in campagna*, where they cultivated the fields and gathered wheat to be used for making bread and pasta. She assisted her father in law, Giovan Battista, with his job, making floor mats.

In 1948, Maria and her children received word from the Red Cross, as Nonna Giuseppa did, that Bernardo had survived the war. Bernardo had located his family through the Vatican in Rome. He sent for them to return to Libya, where they would settle, as many other Sicilians had done by then. A year later in 1949, Daddy's youngest sister Maria was born.

At the tender age of fifteen, Daddy left the shores of Castellamare for the shores of Tripoli. There he continued to work hard to help his family make ends meet. He worked all kinds of jobs and as a result learned so much about so many things. Not only did he know construction and engineering, but he also knew how to speak many languages fluently. He spoke Italian, of course, and the Sicilian dialect. He spoke Spanish and Arabic, too. He would have conversations in Arabic with the man who owned the newsstand around the corner from our building. They would share polite conversation as Daddy purchased his tokens and a newspaper for his train ride to his job at the hospital. When Francesca studied French in junior high school, Daddy would assist her with her homework.

Once he came to America, Dad cooked in a Manhattan restaurant. He could prepare a dish as well as any *nonna* on the block. Everything he made was rich and delicious, and fattening too. Every time Mom started a diet, Dad would tell her, *"Ma va, lascia stare che stai bene. Mangia!"* assuring her that she looked just fine and should enjoy herself and eat. Needless to say Mom's diets never lasted very long.

Sometimes it was really irritating having a father who knew it all. Other times it was really cool to ask him questions because he always knew the answers.

I looked up and saw the small dot that was my father on the Florida horizon. Mom took my hand as I began to tremble. Steadily Daddy made his way back to shore. I exhaled as he stepped out of the water. As the rest of us cheered and clapped he reached for his wife. He embraced Mom with the vigor of a champion accepting his prize. With tears in her eyes Mommy scolded him for soaking her. We stopped for a moment and burst into cheers once more. He had turned fifty-six just one month earlier.

After his victory Daddy was tired. We retreated to the lounge chairs beside the pool as the others took refuge in the air conditioned apartment. I went into the pool to cool off. As I stepped into the water, I was watching Dad. He lay down, closed his eyes and then took a deep breath of the salty air.

I was then inspired to test my own skills as a swimmer. I dived and tumbled in the water. Swimming backwards and forwards, underwater and above the water. This time it was Dad who was watching me. With a grin on his face and an elbow across his head to block the sun from his eyes, he shouted, "Wow you are a fish in the water, just like your father!" My response as I blushed was to giggle. Daddy winked at me.

We had dinner in our room that night, sat around the table and talked for hours. Everyone then retired to their beds. Within a few moments there was silence. All I could hear was some of the others snoring. I lay on the pull-out sofa with Zia Carmela beside me. I looked at her sleeping peacefully and smiled. What a week we all had. It had been a great time for all of us, one that we would never forget. Apparently I fell asleep too because that is the last thing I remember about that night.

The next day we were headed for Orlando to visit my cousin Manny and his family. We would also visit Daddy's cousin Vito. Vito was the son of Daddy's uncle, whom we called Zio Peppino.

Zio Peppino was Nonna Maria's brother. He and his family were the only relatives Daddy had in America from his side of the family. Vito had lived in New York once. I remember visiting him in New Jersey once too. Then he moved to Orlando with his wife and children. We were going to visit my cousins in Orlando then it was back to New York.

We went to Manny's house first. That night Manny and his wife Mickey did not know what to put on the table first. As usual, all we did was eat, drink, and laugh. It was nice spending time with my cousins. It hadn't been easy when one by one they had moved to Florida.

Manny's wife was so funny and affectionate. She could put anyone who was grumpy in a good mood. She was such a sweet girl. When Daddy and Mickey got together they would speak Spanish to each other and pretend to be talking and laughing about everyone else. Then Mickey would lovingly hug Daddy around the neck and kiss his cheek. Daddy would blush, and pat her hand as he told her, *"Gracias, Querida!"*

We spent the night at Manny's house. Lucky me, I got to sleep on the living room floor. Dad was on one side of the sectional and Zio Filippo was on the other. I had to sleep with a pillow over my ears the whole night because my uncle and father made delightful music together with their snoring.

The next day we went to visit Daddy's cousin Vito at his home. His wife picked us up and brought us to their house for dinner. Of course. They too made an appealing spread of antipasti, pasta, meats, followed by fruit, cookies, and cakes for dessert. It was touching to see Daddy and Vito embrace when we first arrived.

They had not seen each other in a long time. Vito was one of the very few blood relatives Daddy had in America. The only others were Vito's brothers and his sisters. When I was a baby and then a little girl, we used to spend more time with Zio Peppino's family. What I remember of them and their families comes from watching the old home movies of our times together. As I got older and Zio Peppino and his wife Zia Peppina passed away, we didn't see the rest of the family that much anymore. Some of them had also moved out of New York by then. As a result, the cousins I know best from Zio's family are his son Vito and his daughters, Piera and Margherita.

In my early twenties I actually became close with Piera, so close that I asked her to read at my wedding. I wanted someone from Daddy's side of the family to have a special part of the ceremony. Piera was touched that I thought of her and I was grateful that she accepted. She wore an extravagant long gown, as if one of her own children were getting married. I had a corsage of lovely white flowers made up for her and asked that she wear it all day. I had the florist put an elegant silver ribbon on the flowers, which brought out the glinting sequins on her gown. She proudly wore that corsage for the ceremony and the entire reception, for she felt honored and special, as I had hoped she would.

At the dinner table that day Vito asked about everyone back home: Ben, Maria, Josephine, and especially Francesca. Francesca was Vito's favorite. Daddy told Vito we were preparing for Francesca's wedding in the fall, and that there was so much to do. Vito turned to me and asked, *"E te signorina, c'è qualche fidanzato?"* because he wanted to know if I too had a fiancé or a boyfriend. I did not answer but felt my face get warm at the question.

Daddy jumped in, *"C'è il boyfriend, ma pensa che suo padre non sa niente. Percio non lo dice,"* thus revealing to his cousin that there was a boyfriend we could not discuss, since he was playing along with my thinking my own father didn't know about him.

I quickly changed the subject by turning to Vito's wife and saying, "Oh Margaret, I love your home. It's beautiful." Daddy and Vito exchanged looks and laughed.

We had a nice time at Vito's house that day and it was sad to see it end. Daddy and his cousin embraced once more. Both their eyes were shining from emotion as they said goodbye with a kiss on both cheeks. One of them said, *"Ci vediamo presto, va bene,"* giving assurance that they would see each other soon. Only that was the last time they saw each other.

The first thing I did when we returned to New York was call that boyfriend Dad was talking about, Joey. Joey and I started dating when I was fifteen years old. He was a year and a half older than me. I had a crush on him a whole year before he asked me out. We had kissed once when I was fourteen years old. After the first time we met, he asked around about me, but some of my guy friends told him to leave me alone. "She's a nice girl," they told him.

He did leave me alone for a little while but not for very long. I was a freshman and he was a sophomore at the same high school. His homeroom was across the hall from mine. I would see him every couple of weeks walking with a new girl. Every time they would hug he would wink at me while the girl's back was turned. I would shake my head and laugh. Feeling my face redden, I would walk quickly into the classroom.

One day after school everyone walked up to the local middle school to see some of our friends. Joey was up there, too. We were talking and joking around with everyone else. He stayed near me the whole time. Whenever he spoke to me, he would touch my elbow or touch my cheek. "You're beautiful," he told me. I just looked at my friend but then she turned and walked away. Joey and I were now standing there a short distance from everyone else. We just kept talking about nothing, really. Then some of our friends started to leave, including the girls that I was with. Joey straightened up from the car he was leaning against and before I had time to protest, (which I had no intention of doing) he kissed me. It was only a second or two but he kissed me. I felt the burning in my cheeks he had touched only a few minutes ago.

He asked for my phone number, hastily wrote it down on his notebook and said he would call me. I felt nervous and exhilarated at the same time. Then he walked in one direction to catch up with his friends and I walked in the other direction to catch up with mine. I got to the corner and ran down the block as I called to them, "Wait! Wait for me!" They were clapping when I got closer. "I kissed him!" I yelled. "I finally kissed him!" I floated home on a cloud that day. I stayed home all night waiting for his call. But the phone did not ring.

The next day at school it seemed we were just friends again. It was as though the kiss never happened. I was upset but I would not let Joey know that.

Eight months and a few girlfriends later, Joey waited for me after school to ask me out. He stood there until I got out of my last class and said hello to me. We sat on a stoop and just talked. He tried to kiss me again but this time I pulled away. "I don't think so," I told him.

He smiled and moved away. "Okay, that's all right," he said.

I just smiled at him and shook my head. He asked me out this time. He asked me to be his girlfriend. I was so happy but still a little mad at him, so I made him wait. Three hours. Then I answered yes. "Finally!" he said.

I opened up my arms to him and said "Okay, now you can kiss me." So he did. This time it was longer and sweeter. Those kisses and that face made me fall in love.

We went out all through that spring and summer. When I turned Sweet Sixteen, Joey bought me a gold ankle bracelet with two ruby hearts in the center and wings on the sides. The wings had our names engraved on them. On the back of one wing was engraved the date we started going out.

I tried to hide the bracelet from Dad but he noticed. When Mom planned a little get together for my birthday with my friends, Dad was sure to say, "No boys!" before either of us even asked. So I just invited a couple of my girlfriends over for cake and pictures. I danced with Daddy in the living room since I did not have a party at a hall, as some of my friends did. Fran put the forty-five on the record player, *Sixteen candles…she's only sixteen but she's my teenage queen…* Daddy and I were laughing and had tears in our eyes too. At least I had that dance.

I knew it was hard for Daddy to accept that his youngest daughter had a boyfriend. One time after an argument, Joey had roses delivered to the apartment. Dad saw my face when I told Mom, "They're for me, Mommy."

My parents assumed the roses were from Francesca's boyfriend, since Francesca was seven years older than I. "Oh," Mommy said. She walked into the kitchen and left it at that. As I walked into my room with the card in my hand I heard Daddy mumbling something in Sicilian to Mommy. In response to this, Mom asked, *"E che ci posso fare?"* wanting to know what he thought she could do. Dad did not answer. He just sat in his chair with a grimace on his face. I thought it best to stay in my room for a while. I didn't want to aggravate the situation by having Daddy ask questions, but I was both happy and nervous. I was happy about the roses that Joey had sent me, but nervous at the look of annoyance on my father's face.

A local club opened up that summer and you only had to be eighteen to get in. With a lot of makeup, fancy clothes, and fake I.D., everyone was there every weekend. Everyone but me, that is. I was never allowed to go out like the rest of the girls. I had to be home at ten o'clock on a Saturday! My friends were still getting ready for the club at ten o'clock. I was livid.

Joey was working at a restaurant that summer, and sometimes did not get home from work until nine thirty or ten o'clock. I barely got to see him. One Saturday afternoon I asked Daddy if just this once I could stay out until at least midnight. "No! Ten o'clock." That was it.

Still, I protested, "But Daddy my friends are just going dancing at ten o'clock. I can never go with them." Daddy pointed out the stereo system that he and Mom bought me for my sixteenth birthday.

"You want to dance?" he asked, "Here, right here, you have the music here. You turn the lights on and off like this with the switch and you dance. All night you can dance!"

I stormed into the living room where Mommy was. Dad followed behind me and plunked himself down in his chair. Mom looked from her husband to her daughter. Then she threw her hands up in the air and went into the kitchen. I had no ally this time.

"Ten o'clock!" Dad barked at me. "Take it or leave it!" I stamped my feet and cried.

"Daddy my boyfriend gets out of work at ten o'clock. I never get to see him. It's not fair!" I slapped my hand over my mouth. Mom was standing in the doorway between the kitchen and the living room. She and I stared at each other, shocked that those words just came out of my mouth and afraid at what would happen next.

Daddy started to get up from his chair and I ran. As fast as I could. I ran to my room and locked the door behind me. I heard Dad screaming something in Sicilian as he walked to my room with a heavy footfall. He pounded on the door and yelled at me, "Your **who**, your **what**? You tell your **boyfriend** to find someone else because **you**, *figia mia*, are *never* going out again!"

That night I told Joey over the phone what happened with Dad. Of course, I did not get to go out at all that night. I was crying, angry, and frustrated as I told him the whole story. But Joey was laughing when I told him what Daddy said about the stereo and dancing.

31

"He's a funny guy, your father. He's a wise ass. I like him already!"

"Oh I'm glad you think it's funny. I may never see sunlight again!"

Thank goodness Daddy worked the 12:00 p.m.to 8:00 p.m. shift at the hospital. In an effort to protect me, Mom would threaten death if I got home a minute past eight o'clock. During junior year in high school I could not take it anymore. Joey and I had been seeing each other after school for almost two years by then. Finally I took a deep breath and begged Daddy if he would meet him. After a little persuasion from Josephine, Mommy, and Francesca, Dad finally agreed to meet my boyfriend. Benny did not want to hear that his baby sister was bringing home a boyfriend already. Maria I was too nervous to even tell I *had* a boyfriend. She was almost as bad as Daddy when it came to me. "You're not too young?" she asked me when she found out. I knew she would not help my case with this one.

This was the deal Dad gave me. "Bring the guy here. If I don't like him or I don't like his family, you will never see him again. You go to school and straight home. If your mother lets you go out when I am at work then she is in trouble too. *Hai capito*? Understand?"

I shook my head in agreement. Mommy was standing behind him and rolling her eyes when he made the comment about *her* being in trouble. He turned and noticed she was standing there. "*Perchè mi guardi?*" he asked her, wanting to know why she was looking at him. She walked away and waved her hand at him.

"*Neanche sto guardare a te,*" she replied, denying his accusation. Daddy shook his head and smiled, knowing Mommy was making faces at him from the kitchen.

And so it went. Joey came over. He was polite and said all the right things. When Joey mentioned marriage, Dad sent Mom and me out of the room. We were eavesdropping from the foyer. I was shaking and Mom was holding me with a finger on her lip to keep me quiet. Joey had nerve, I'll give him that. He explained to Dad how he and every guy in the neighborhood respected me because I was "a nice girl." My legs almost buckled. "I want to marry your daughter one day," he told Daddy.

I heard Dad moving around in his chair as it rocked on the linoleum. Crawling out of his skin probably. They were speaking to each other in Sicilian. Good move on Joey's part. But Dad dismissed any further discussion of marriage. "Let's save that conversation for when she graduates high school. For now you could see each other. On the weekends. You come over during the week if you like and have dinner with our family. Not too late when she has school. When you go out together I want my daughter in the house by midnight. A minute before is okay. A minute after is too late. *D'accordo?*" Joey extended his hand and they shook on Daddy's terms.

"*D'accordo.*" Joey agreed. By then Mom and I were going into cardiac arrest.

The next few months were great. Joey was part of the family. Everyone liked him, even my brother Ben and my sister Maria. Joey and Daddy hung out sometimes when I was not even around. I think they went to the city together once by train. Another time I came home from work and found them out cold in the living room.

I had come home from my shift at the bakery. No one else was at home. I smelled like bread and had powdered sugar all over my smock and hair. I opened the door to the apartment and saw Joey laying on the couch and Daddy on his recliner. They were both asleep. There was an empty gallon of wine on the floor beside Dad. There were sauce-stained dishes on the table. "Look at this!" I said aloud. They did not budge. I shook my head and let them sleep.

But Joey and I didn't have a perfect situation. The trouble started right before I graduated high school. Nonna Giuseppa died that year. Joey and I were arguing a lot. The emotion of Nonna's death, the pressure of graduation. Just everything. For these and a number of small and big reasons, we split up. My heart was broken. Ten million tiny pieces. I missed my prom. I missed Joey so much.

Then Joey and I got back together. But we split up again. Dad could not take it anymore. That July he sent me away to Florida with Zia Adriana and Zio Filippo, who were going there for a month. The same place we would go together one year later. Dad entrusted me with his friends and their daughter Concetta. Daddy wanted *me* out of New York, and *Joey* out of my heart.

I shared a room with Connie and her son Jeremy. Her husband came on some of the weekends because of work. Jeremy was so little. He would cry out at night, "Aaaaaaapple juuuuuice!" and Concetta and I would laugh out loud because he was so cute. He could not say "Susie" so he called me "Suesha." The name kind of stuck when I get together with their family.

I would stay up at night with Connie, telling her about Joey and me. She always listened and tried to make me feel better. Connie was certain that Joey and I loved each other. She said the time apart would help us realize what was really important to us. "Things will work out," she reassured me. Sometimes Zia would find me walking by myself on the beach in a quiet daze. Other times she would come and get me as I sat alone on a swing right beyond the boardwalk. When I would talk to her she would just put her arm around my shoulders and walk with me back to our room. She would tell Mom on the phone how sad I looked. Then I would hear her asking if Joey had come by to ask for me or not.

Mom told Zia what happened one time when Joey did come by to ask about me. Joey rang the bell and Daddy buzzed him in. He looked down the three flights of stairs and saw Joey standing there. When Joey asked if he could see me Daddy said, "She's not here. I sent her to Florida," and he started to walk back into the apartment. "When is she coming back?" Joey asked.

"She's not coming back!" Daddy replied. "She is going to stay there for college." *SLAM!!!* went the door to the apartment. Apparently Daddy went straight to the bedroom and watched from the window as Joey left the building and walked toward the corner.

Zia Adriana made a sad face. *"Mi sento male"* she said, because she felt so bad. *"È un bravo ragazzo, ancora ragazzi sono,"* which, in Zia's wisdom, meant that Joey was a nice boy and that the two of us were just kids.

I could not hear Mom's reaction to her best friend's sympathy. Zio Filippo never spoke to me about Joey. He just patted me on the shoulder when Joey's name was mentioned. Zio is a quiet man that way. Whenever I've told him, "I love you, Zio" he always smiles and says, "Oh thank you, me too." I smile back at him and kiss his cheek.

At the end of August, right before Labor Day, I came back to New York. I saw Joey that very night. I was in a car with my friend Lisa. He stopped us and I got out to speak with him. There goes that face again. That gorgeous face that I could never resist He kissed me before I even said hello. My eyes filled with tears and I pulled away. "I have to go, Joey. I can't do this." I got back in the car and cried as Lisa drove away. When we pulled into Lisa's driveway later that night, there he was, standing with a big teddy bear and a card in his hands. Leaning on a car just like the first time we kissed. I did not refuse his kiss that night either.

Dad forbid me to see Joey when I came home from Florida, so for a while we stayed friends. Mostly we just talked on the phone. But sometimes we saw each other and kissed some more. I was working full time by then. Late hours. I only went out sometimes on the weekends. My mind was on Joey all the time, though. I could not stay away.

Eventually we just had to see each other and started going out again. I could not tell Dad, so we kept it quiet. Eventually Dad found out about us through the neighborhood grapevine, but he never mentioned anything to me. He wanted no part of it. He was upset with Joey for breaking up with me that summer and was angry that he had heard his daughter cry behind her locked bedroom door. When he walked past me, I'd keep my head down to avoid his eyes. But then he'd lift my face toward his with a finger under my chin. I would look at him and he'd say nothing, but he would just put an arm around me and kiss my cheek. Then I would go back into my room.

Joey wanted to speak with Daddy. He wanted to apologize and make things right. I told him to wait. In the meantime we sneaked around together.

I never did make it to college after high school. The deadlines for registration had come and gone while I was in Florida. I had not put much effort into it in the first place, anyway. Now, as an adult, if I could go back in time to find myself as a teenager, I would slap myself in the face and get myself into college right after high school. I should have listened to my parents. But back then I just wanted to make money and be independent. I wanted to be able to buy the things I couldn't have before. I wanted to help my parents and be able to afford special gifts for Francesca's wedding. They had done so much for me. Like many young people, I was thinking of instant gratification instead of long-term career goals.

Delaying my education seemed harmless enough, but then life got in the way of my plans. That's what happened to me. Six months turned into ten years and six months, and I did not go to college until I was twenty-eight years old.

In the fall following my high school graduation, I got a full time job as a receptionist at a full service wedding center. That came in handy because Francesca was getting married the following year. The plan was at first to take just six months off to work. Then six months turned into a year. By that time, Francesca was preparing for the wedding and I would be her maid of honor. I planned to go to college after the wedding.

I knew that Fran and her fiancé were paying for the wedding themselves, and through my job I was able to get them all kinds of discounts on their wedding services. I made sure they got the best photographer; I selected their baby pictures for the wedding video, and even spent hours choosing their wedding song. Fran did pick out her own wedding favors, though.

With every paycheck I got that summer, I put something aside for the favors, and one day came home with the receipt for those favors, marked **"Paid in Full"** in red ink. In our kitchen, I put a hand on Fran's shoulder and slipped that receipt in front of her face. She looked at it twice and took it out of my hand. Then she looked at it more closely and started to cry with gratitude. We hugged and I cried too. Daddy kissed Fran on the back of her head and gave me a pat on the back. *"Hai fatto bene,"* he told me, approving of what I had done.

That August I turned nineteen. My birthday came and went quietly, as everyone was so busy with the wedding. We had Fran's bridal shower a few weeks before my birthday. The wedding day was approaching quickly.

When my parents had the family come over for cake and coffee, everyone gave me cards with money inside. Mom and Dad gave me a card with money too, even though they had already paid my airfare for Florida just a couple of months earlier.

In the days after my birthday, things were quiet at home. One afternoon when I got home from work, Mom and Fran were out doing wedding errands, so it was just Dad and me. I was in the kitchen and Dad was in his bedroom. Then I heard his voice call me into the living room. He seemed so serious that I thought I was in trouble. *Here it comes*, I thought.

I approached him with caution as he took my hand. *What did I do?* I wondered. Daddy, who could clearly read my thoughts, laughed at the expression on my face. "You're not in trouble," he reassured me. I was embarrassed at my obviously guilty conscience. When he let go of my hand, there was a surprise in it — a pair of gold hoop earrings. The kind that Daddy liked me to wear because of my long curly hair.

"These are for me?" I asked him.

He laughed again. *"No sono le mie! Ti piacciano?"* sarcastically but good naturedly telling me no, they were *his*! But did I *like* them?

I gave him a silly look. "You and Mommy did so much already, *Papà*." He took both my hands as he put the earrings on one of the oak end tables near the couch.

"This is my gift for my little girl," he said tenderly. "You never know tomorrow. This way you remember *che tuo padre ti vuole bene,*" he said, making sure I knew that he loved me.

I could not speak. I just embraced his neck and kissed my father's face a million times. Now we were both laughing. "I could never forget you Daddy. I love you too much, even when you drive me crazy!" We laughed as he gave me a mock dirty look, and then we hugged again. Tightly. Holding on a moment longer.

I take those earrings out every year on my birthday. I sometimes wear them for the day. Other times I just hold them in the palm of my hand as I did the day Daddy gave them to me. I will never forget that my father loved me. How could I? I think back and imagine what was going through Daddy's mind. Did he suspect something was wrong? Did he just have a bad feeling?

Starting in the early spring of that year, Daddy often suffered from terrible headaches. His warm olive complexion would suddenly turn ashen. He would sit back in his chair, tilt his head back and close his eyes. If we fussed over him it only made him angry. Mom nagged him about seeing a doctor. "After my daughter's wedding I go!" he'd snap at her. The wedding was a month away.

I felt so guilty that day when Daddy gave me those earrings. I had been such a brat, pouting around the house, but I couldn't help it. I was so angry with him. I wanted to bring Joey to Fran's wedding and was too nervous to ask Daddy's permission myself. I got Francesca to do it for me. Daddy never yelled at Fran. He had no problem yelling at Benny, Josephine, and me, but for some reason he was a little more cautious with Francesca and Maria's feelings. In any case, it was Francesca's wedding. I figured he wouldn't refuse one of her wishes, right? Then for some reason I thought about *The Godfather.* The movie starts with Marlon Brando playing Vito Corleone. Vito's daughter Connie is getting married at his home. All these people are coming in and out of his office requesting favors from the Godfather. Then in one scene, the Tom Hagen character tells his wife, "No Sicilian can refuse a favor on the day of his daughter's wedding."

Cool! I thought. Daddy can't say no to Francesca because *she's* the one getting married. Then I questioned my thoughts. Maybe he can't refuse favors from *other* people on the day his daughter is married but he could still refuse his daughter's requests. How does that work, I wonder? Well, back to reality. Daddy was not a *Don* in the Mafia. The only family he was in charge of was ours. There were no rules or codes he had to follow, only his own.

I was in my room the night Francesca found the courage to ask Dad. I left the door open in hopes of hearing their conversation.

"Daddy I need to ask you something," Fran said. "It's a favor for my wedding. Can Susie please bring Joey to the wedding?" she asked meekly.

"NO!" That was Dad's response.

"But Daddy, please. You already know they are seeing each other. Susie is my maid of honor. I want her to be happy. Please, *Papà.*" I could picture beads of sweat forming on my sister's forehead.

Dad sat up in his chair. Even if you were deaf you would have understood his answer to Francesca's question. "I let that guy in this house. *My* house. Even though my daughter was too young. (*Hello! Dad married my mother when <u>she</u> was sixteen!*) He sat right there and told me he loved your sister. 'I want to marry your daughter,' he told me. I treat him as part of this family. My family. I invite him to my home, to my table. I even let him go out with my little girl, *alone.* Then he breaks my baby's heart. He made her cry!

No!" he shouted, "No! That's my answer, no!"

For a moment, Fran pondered her next move, her next tactic. "*Papà*," she ventured, "They are just kids. They had a few arguments and they broke up for a little while. They got back together. Come on, Daddy, *please*."

The eyes narrowed as his finger pointed up into the air. "*Tua sorella la perdonato, io no però!*" pronouncing that while *I* had forgiven Joey, *he* had not.

My poor sister was red-faced as she came into my room. I held my hand up in defeat. "I heard." Fran caressed my hair and said, "I'm so sorry honey, I really tried." God knows she was no match for Daddy. Maybe I should have asked Josephine to ask him. He was being so damn stubborn, so, so, *so*, SICILIAN! He was not ready to forgive Joey yet. Not the boy who broke his baby daughter's heart. Even though I was happy now that things were going so well for Joey and me.

I thought my father and I had an unspoken agreement that Daddy knew, as I walked around the house smiling again, that Joey and I were back together. We just never discussed it. But with time a girl learns to pick her battles with a Sicilian father. And this battle would have to wait.

The end of that summer brought Francesca's wedding. It would take place on our mother's forty-ninth birthday. I would be maid of honor, and Maria, Josephine, and Fran's best friend would be bridesmaids. The color scheme for Francesca's wedding was Black & White, which was a chic trend in the late 1980s. We girls wore black and white slim-fitting gowns. The invitations were black and white. The balloons were black and white. Even the ribbons on our bouquets were black and white.

Mom was furious when we came home from the bridal shop. "*No, non può essere!*" she said in horror, insisting that this just could *not* be. According to Mom and Italian superstition, black was for funerals, not weddings. Francesca choosing black and white for her wedding color scheme was *Malaugurio,* an invitation for bad luck. But Fran's mind was made up. Even Mom's foreboding would not change her mind about the colors for the wedding.

By early September Fran was getting crazy, as brides do. My parents and I took care of cleaning the house. Maria helped too. Josephine was pregnant at the time with her fourth child, so her abilities were limited. Daddy cleaned our paneled walls one by one with his own hands. The rest of us took down curtains, washed windows, put up new blinds and curtains. We dusted everything in sight. The house was spotless.

I started getting tips put on my nails a few weeks before the wedding. Mom and Dad did not let me do anything that would ruin my expensive manicures. They knew I could not afford them to begin with. I just wanted everything to be perfect for Francesca's wedding, including the way I looked. A few months before the wedding, I lost thirty pounds, eating only small portions and cutting down on pasta and bread. Imagine *that* in my house. No pasta. It was hard.

Every night I was in front of the television doing aerobics. Daddy would eat his dinner, pasta, or steak with fried potatoes, and watch me exercise. *"Brava!"* he would yell from the kitchen. Applauding my efforts. *"Meglio ora che sei giovane. Se non ti guardi chi sa un giorno ti devi mettere i mutandi della Mamma!"* advising that it's better to do this when one is young so as not to end up in "your mother's underwear." It sounds better in Italian.

Sweating, I would roll on my side from my sit-up position, unable to catch my breath because I was laughing too hard. Mom would take a dish towel and hit Daddy with it, and he would have to drink half a glass of wine to avoid choking on his food. His whole body shook when he laughed.

I did my mother's laundry just the other day. As I folded her underwear, I thought of my father's words. I couldn't help but laugh. My husband asked me what I was laughing about but I just shook my head and kept the moment for myself. What a memory this was. You had to be there.

But this was Francesca's time. Her moment. It had to be great, special, like her. Fran had done so much for everyone else, including, and perhaps especially, me. When we were in school, our older sisters were already married. Mom and Dad both worked but still struggled to make ends meet, so when Fran was old enough to start working, she always bought me clothes and toys. When I got old enough, she bought me books and make-up.

Ben was in the Army and got married before Fran did, so there was a while when Fran and I were the only two kids living at home. When I was in high school and Fran was already working full time, we'd have a "sister date" every Friday. I would meet her around the corner by the train station and we'd walk across the street to this German diner on the corner. We each ate a pizza burger deluxe then shared a huge piece of chocolate pudding pie. On Saturday mornings we walked on the avenue for hours shopping, and she'd always treat me to something for keeping her company. I loved my big sister. She was smart and beautiful and she cared about me. Even when I was already a teenager, Fran held my hand to cross the street. Come to think of it, when I was pregnant with my son, my sister was holding my hand to cross the street. Some things never change. Francesca was my favorite person in the whole world, even when we argued, as sisters do.

Only two things caused Fran and me to argue. She would get so angry with me for wearing her clothes without permission. I would wait until she went to work then put her clothes on for school. After all, I wanted to look good too. She actually had Daddy put a lock on her closet my junior year of high school. But once Francesca and I got our own rooms and I was able to buy my own clothes, we had nothing more to argue about.

At night, I would throw pillows at Fran because she always snored loudly or talked in her sleep. Once she was fighting with someone in one of her dreams. She yelled out, "You witch!" and started kicking the bottom of my bed from the bottom bunk. I started crying and screaming out for Daddy, "*Papà, Papà, Franca mi sta dare calci! Ma detto una brutta parola!*" tattling on my sister for kicking me and calling me an ugly name.

Daddy ran into our room, startled at my screaming. "*Cosa sta sucedere? Perchè stai gridare? Mai fatto venire un attaco di cuore! Franca che stai fare? Stai fare male a tua sorella!*" which was a very long way of scolding us for yelling, maybe causing a heart attack, and Fran hurting the little one. Fran and I laugh about that now.

But now she was getting married and the whole family was getting nervous. That morning, our apartment was full of people – Fran's best friend, us sisters, our parents, my brother. Our three nephews looked so precious in their tuxedos. Even one of Mommy's cousins, Maria Rosa, had come from Torino, Italy to attend the wedding. It promised to be a real New York-style Italian bash.

By now, Fran was officially insane and was driving everyone else crazy too. She hated her hair. She hated her make up. As any decent maid of honor would, I tried to break the tension and calm her down. I teased her, saying, "Fran, should I slap you? Calm down. I'll slap you if I have to!" She stared at me. Then she looked around at everyone else. Suddenly the dam had broken and there were tears everywhere. She was hysterical. "Oh man, Fran," I said, "I was just kidding! I would never slap you for real. I was trying to make you laugh!" I felt so bad.

"No," she sobbed, "I can't believe today I'm getting married."

Mom reminded her, "Franca, we've been planning this wedding for more than a year already." She went to Fran and smoothed back her hair. She checked Fran's headpiece.

"I know, Ma, but oh, my God, it's *today*!" Tears then turned to laughter for all of us.

My brother Benny saved us all once the photographer arrived. He started making jokes and we could not help but laugh. He was hiding it well, my brother, hiding his anxiety over Francesca's wedding. He and Fran are only fifteen months apart. They have always been close and even grew up with the same friends. Her friends had crushes on Ben. His friends regarded Fran as Benny's little sister. In high school the guys called Fran and our cousin Antoinette "The Untouchables." No one was allowed to go near them. If any guy tried to hang around Fran or Antoinette, both Benny and cousin Tony would be up at school the next day. The surprise of their very presence was a threat in itself. Even now, on the day of Fran's wedding, Ben felt protective of his younger sister. He was hiding his emotions, as he usually did, behind a sense of humor. We know that his heart is bigger than he will ever admit.

Once the photographer was finished shooting, we headed for the church. As maid of honor I got to ride with my father and the bride. We were cruising along quietly in a white antique Rolls Royce when Daddy finally panicked. He turned to Fran and was babbling nervously. "*Franca, sei sicura?*" he asked, wanting to know if she were sure. "The wedding. The marriage. *Tutte cose!* Everything! Are you sure? If it's the money you spent I will give it back to you. I take a loan from work and I pay you back everything you spent. Tell me the truth, Franca! *La verità voglio!* I will tell the driver right now to turn the car around. We go home you get some clothes. I send you away for a little while. No wedding, *niente matrimonio se non sei sicura!*" he assured her - no wedding if you're not absolutely sure.

Then Dad took a breath. Imagine, twenty minutes before your wedding ceremony. Fran looked at me and I looked at her. Dad was ready to go home and send Fran away if she was not ready for the wedding or the marriage. It was silent in the car for a moment. Fran and I were still trying to comprehend what just happened. Dad was just holding Francesca's hand, waiting for her answer. Then she spoke, "*Papà, sono sicura*. I'm sure, Daddy. I promise." Dad nodded his head and took out a handkerchief to wipe the sweat off his brow.

"Va bene, Gioia, va bene," giving his "okay." He never mentioned it again.

* * *

When I told Mom later about what happened in the limousine, she explained to me why Daddy said all those things to Francesca. Apparently, Mom told Daddy about Fran's sudden panic on the morning of the wedding. Daddy, knowing that my sister was always trying to do the right thing, thought perhaps his daughter was unsure about the marriage. He knew she would not want to embarrass the family by calling off the wedding at the last minute. Francesca was very quiet with her feelings, always keeping her emotions to herself. Dad or Mom would always have to persuade Francesca to talk when they sensed something was wrong with her. As bright and mature as Fran was, she was always childlike in that way. That's why in our family we always felt we had to protect her, even if she were not asking for protection. We were never quite sure what Francesca was really feeling.

Despite the morning drama, the wedding went on as planned. We got to the church and everyone was outside waiting for the bride to arrive. So many people, family and friends. The groom and best man waiting inside. This was it. My sister getting married. Now *I* was ready for an anxiety attack. *My Francesca, my big sister. Oh, God. Okay, I can get through this.* As excited and supportive as I had been through the planning of Francesca's wedding, I had been secretly dreading this day for I knew that Fran would leave our home and more important, she would be leaving me. Tears rose to my eyes but I bit my lip and took a deep breath. Daddy must have sensed that I was getting emotional and I felt his hand on my shoulder. But I could not look back at him. The bridal party was already walking down the aisle, couple by couple, as I tried to remember what was happening. Then it was my turn. I walked down the aisle by myself. *Was I staggering? Am I walking straight? Don't fall, please don't fall.* Despite my momentary selfishness over losing Francesca, I was still determined that this moment be perfect for her. The last thing I wanted to do was tumble down the aisle. My dress and shoes were a little tight, which made being graceful a bit difficult. But that diet I had followed paid off, and I walked down that aisle in a size six. I could almost *feel* Francesca and Daddy, both naturally skinny, exchanging looks and grinning behind me.

I did it. I got there. My future brother-in-law smiled at me when I made it to the altar. I smiled back. I loved him. He was always kind to me. But still, here was the man who was taking my sister away from me.

Okay, think positive. Then the wedding march began to play. There she was, my beautiful sister. Even more exquisite than I had ever seen her. Her long, golden hair was just a little wavy that day, thanks to those spiral curlers she bought. Her round, amber eyes were sparkling. She looked like one of those models from *Modern Bride*. Even her slender figure looked picture perfect in a mermaid-style gown. *Yet*, I thought, *she looks like she will break into pieces if I touch her*. I got choked up. My father did his duty. He walked his daughter down that aisle, his back straight and his head held high. He lifted the blusher off Fran's face and kissed her on both cheeks. Without speaking a word, he took her hand and then her fiancé's hand and joined them together. He patted them both on the back and turned to sit.

Daddy sat in his seat beside his wife and did not flinch during the whole wedding ceremony. Mommy took his hand and held it. We managed to get through the next thirty minutes. It was still hard to think of Fran as not living at home anymore. Francesca had been the baby of the house for seven years until I came along. The two of us kind of shared the position of the babies in the family. That's one of the reasons we were always so close. But now one of us was leaving the family nest. It felt like the end of an era.

My brother-in-law and Fran were so nervous that they kept laughing during the entire ceremony. The priest cleared his throat several times in disapproval. I guess he didn't think it was funny. The rest of us did, though.

Then the groom kissed his bride and then they were *Mr. and Mrs.* Everyone clapped as the couple made its way toward the church doors. Outside the church, I had one of my younger cousins give out the silk roses filled with birdseed, which I had made up before the wedding. Another surprise gift for Francesca.

Fran had been home the day I brought the birdseed flowers into the house. I rang the bell and she buzzed me in. Then from the bottom of the stairs I started shouting, "Special delivery for Francesca!"

Fran saw me with this basket in my hand that I could barely carry up three flights of stairs. "Susie, what is that? *Papà, Mamma, guarda!*" she said, urging our parents to look. I got to the top of the stairs and Fran moved out of the way. I put the basket and silk roses on the table and took one out to show Fran. "Look, sister," I said.

The ribbons had Fran's name and her fiancé's name engraved on them, along with a cute poem. Fran took one out of my hand, looked at it and started to cry. Mom cried too. So did I. Daddy was laughing at us. His eyes were shiny. Josephine came through the door. "What happened?" she asked. Mom explained.

"Look what your sister bought for the wedding. They're roses with the seed inside to throw at Franca when she gets married."

Josephine picked up a flower. "Oh how nice! You didn't buy *me* flowers when I got married."

I made a face at her. "Uh, maybe because I was nine years *old* when you got married!"

We all started laughing, including Fran, as she embraced me once more. "They are beautiful," Josephine said. "Next time I get married you could buy them for me."

Again me, with the face. "Yeah, okay, Jo. As you walk around with your fourth kid still in your stomach!" Josephine made a sarcastic face back at me and stuck her tongue out at me. Fran was laughing now.

"I'm gonna miss this," she said.

We went to a studio after the ceremony to take pictures. The photographer was telling us jokes to make us smile for the pictures. While we waited for him to finish taking formal shots of the bride and groom alone, we were getting restless. The guys were loosening their ties and we girls were slipping off our shoes. It had been a long day for our nephews, but God bless them, they were still in good spirits. Everyone was occupying them by giving them money for the vending machines. Some chips and soda kept the boys happy and they got a kick out of riding in a limousine.

By the time we got to the reception we were exhausted. But not for long. We had some food and a few drinks and we were ready for a party. The hall was a nice Italian place on Coney Island. It was there that my brother-in-law had proposed to Fran and where the couple loved to go while they were dating. We all made a grand entrance, forming an arc with our bouquets and ribbons for the happy couple to walk through. Then they danced to the wedding song that I had chosen.

Next came good food, fine liquor, and great music. By the time we all had a couple of drinks and some appetizers, the D.J. played an Italian song, *"Ti Amo."* My cousin Tony has a nice voice and that's one of his favorite songs, so he got up first. Ben stood next to him and the two of them were singing together into a microphone. Then one by one, most of the cousins got up and started singing too. We stood in a circle with our arms around one another, screwing up the words every so often. You could barely hear the music over our voices. We were totally off key, but in harmony all the same.

My sister had the maitre'd bring out a cake with candles for Mom and we all sang again. Mom's cheeks were flushed and her eyes were twinkling as she tried not to cry. She looked so lovely in her pink gown. People have told me all my life I look like Mom, to which I reply, *"Grazie,"* because Mom has such a pretty face. Dad hated when she wore makeup because he thought she was prettier without it. Although I have my father's eyes, Daddy always told me that like my mother, my eyes smile when I am happy. My eyes would shine and the rest of my face would light up too. Daddy would also tease Mom and me, saying that we had the same pouting lips when we were angry.

Mom still says it was the best birthday she ever had. After the cake, we all made a conga line as the D.J. played "Hands Up!" Then each person went down the line dancing and lifting their hands. When it was Ben's turn he did a "Jackie Gleason" and pulled back his jacket so he could show his stomach wiggling. With that silly grin on his face he made everyone crack up. Ben is a character, my brother. It was a great party. I didn't have a date there but I danced all night anyway. My shoes were under the table by the time the pasta was served.

Then came the best part of the whole affair. Francesca escorted Daddy onto the dance floor. They danced to another Italian song, "*O, My Papà.* The lyrics were so appropriate for Francesca and Daddy. "*O, my Papà, sei l'uomo più adorabile…*" Francesca adored Daddy. She never answered him back and always hugged and kissed him.

Daddy would sometimes call Francesca *Ciccia.* When a man is named Francesco or Frank sometimes people will call him *Ciccio.* Fran was Daddy's *Ciccia.* It was her pet name. Every time Daddy went to Italy to visit his family, Francesca became ill. She would get a fever or a stomachache.

One time when Daddy was away, Francesca was inconsolable. To make her feel better, Mommy scraped up a little money and took Francesca to buy a new coat — even as a kid, Fran loved to shop for clothes. Francesca loved the new coat and was smiling for a little while but before long she was whining again. Mom was beside herself!

Dad came home and felt bad, but was quite amused at his

daughter's loyalty. He went out and bought a record and played it on the record player. *"Daddy's home. Daddy's home….Daddy's home to stay… I'm not a thousand miles away…"* Something like that. It was Francesca's favorite song for a month. Mom was ready to throw the record out the window, but she didn't. She too had missed Dad while he was away.

Francesca tried to be flawless for our parents. She always felt bad about their hard times. They were married so young and had not had their own apartment until they came to America. And now, despite their hard work and sacrifices, they still did not own their own home. Fran wanted so badly to take care of them and make them feel proud of their life and their children. Fran was the first of their children to graduate from high school. She graduated six months early with a Regents diploma. When I went to the same high school, I had one of her teachers. As Ms. Leonardelli read my last name from the roster she asked me, "Do you have a sister named Francesca?"

I smiled in surprise and answered, "Yes, I do." Right then I realized I had to do well in that class. I had a high standard to live up to as Francesca's younger sister. Not only would my teacher expect me to do well, but Daddy had his own standard for me, too, especially because Ms. Leonardelli taught us Italian.

I remember coming home from school one day, so excited because I got a ninety-eight percent on an exam. I showed it to Daddy and explained why the two points were deducted – it was really an oversight on my part when I had read the directions. Dad stood quietly for a moment as he looked over the paper. Then he looked at me with a straight face and said, "You know if you were able to get a ninety-eight percent then you could have gotten one hundred percent." Those words are what kept me up many nights during my time in college. Every time I had to write a paper or I had to study for an exam, I thought of him.

Whenever I had written a paper and thought it was acceptable to hand in, I would remember my father's words. Then I would go and read the whole paper again and edit it once more. On one of my sociology papers the professor wrote *A+++ Excellent Writing*. I guess you could say it was Daddy who turned me into a bit of a perfectionist. Some could debate that Daddy was a little harsh by saying what he did, but as an adult, I am grateful Daddy challenged my abilities. It's part of the reason I am who I am now as a wife, a mother, an educator, and certainly as a writer.

My sister Francesca was also on a pedestal in our father's eyes. Daddy always bragged about how beautiful she was, and he'd frequently mention how she had been approached by a talent scout asking her if she was interested in modeling. Francesca of course was too modest to accept such an offer, and her modesty added to her beauty. Daddy was so proud of how Francesca could speak English, Italian, and French, "all very gracefully," he would add.

Once Francesca started working full time, she earned more money than both our parents' salaries combined. Right before she got married, Francesca and some colleagues had gone into business for themselves while still working another part-time job. Francesca would help Mom with the household expenses and quietly slip Daddy some extra money for his hobbies. She knew he loved to buy all the latest music. He loved renting videos too. Westerns and Italian movies. He would go down to Brooklyn or Little Italy and buy the latest music from the yearly Sanremo festivals in Italy. Fran would put money in the drawer of Daddy's nightstand when he wasn't looking. She would slip money into his jacket pockets. In time he would find it and know exactly where it came from. Daddy took some of the money Fran gave him and shared it with Josephine.

Josephine and her husband had three little boys. Because Josephine stayed home with them and didn't work, things were difficult financially. Now they were expecting their fourth child. Daddy would always ask Fran's permission first, and Fran never said no or got upset. She would do anything for Josephine's boys. We all felt that those boys were our boys too. All of ours.

As Fran and my father danced that night, I wondered what my sister was thinking. Neither of them cried. As luminous as Daddy's eyes appeared, he just kept smiling from ear to ear as he and his *Ciccia* danced, the two of them chuckling. Fran made everyone laugh by taking off her shoes in the middle of the dance, pointing out how she and Daddy were almost the same height. In her heels she was just a little bit taller than Daddy. It was funny and everyone was laughing through their moist eyes. Francesca hugged Daddy a million times and kept kissing his face. With every kiss, his smile grew wider and brighter. They looked blissful together. It was a truly glorious moment. I will always envy my sister for that dance, although I know how much she deserved it.

After we celebrated a little more, the reception came to an end. It was time to say goodnight to the newlyweds. Everyone crowded around them as soon as the last song started, forming a line beside the dais table, envelopes in hand. I remember Fran giving out those favors for which I had so proudly paid.

Finally there was a break in the line. I raced to my sister's side, kissed my new brother-in-law and in a very *"Goodfellas"* voice I said, "Take care of my sister!" He laughed at me and shook his head, kissing my cheek as he reassured me he would. Then Francesca and I stood there face to face. My voice escaped me. There were no words from either of us. We just embraced so tightly, neither of us letting go for a while. I kissed her face and she kissed mine. Then we squeezed hands and I walked away.

When I did look back at my sister, she was wiping a tear from her cheek. A moment later she was smiling again as she said goodnight to the rest of her guests. It was hard to tell that night if my sister's smile was real. Was she happy or was it one of those clenched teeth smiles we need to put on for everyone else's sake? Years later I would get my answer.

When we got home, there were people everywhere again. Some of the relatives came back to the apartment after the reception for one more drink and to congratulate the family. I was exhausted and went to my new room. Sleeping in the big bedroom again, this time by myself. What a relief to take off that tight headpiece. I peeled that slim-fitting dress off my body and changed to sweat pants and a T-shirt.

I knew that despite my exhaustion, I was too wound up to sleep, but I went to lie down anyway. On my pillow was an envelope with my name on it. I recognized the handwriting right away. *Oh, no,* I thought. *Here I go.* As I tore open the envelope I heard the last of the company leaving. Everyone had assumed I was already asleep, so I didn't get up from my bed. I could not wait to read Francesca's letter and wished I had some tissues handy. To the best of my memory here is how it read:

Dear Susie,

Hey, little sister. I know I haven't paid much attention to you lately. I am so sorry. I wanted to spend some "sister" time with you before I got married. Everything just got so crazy the past couple of months. Time went by so quickly.

Susie, you have been such a huge help with the wedding. I don't know what I would have done without you. You helped Mommy and Daddy with the house too. Those flowers and the favors. I know it was so hard for you to pay for all that. But you did for me.

I don't know if I ever told you this, but you are the greatest little sister in the whole world. I am going to miss you so much. I will miss living at home with you. We have had great times together.

Just remember I will always be your big sister. It doesn't matter where I live. I will always look out for you. I will always love you. You will always be my baby, my treasure!

Do me a favor, Sue. Take care of Mommy and Daddy. I know sometimes they make us crazy. But please just let them talk. Especially Daddy. I know he will be on your back even more now that you're the only one at home. Have patience. You know how he is with us. Just be there for both of them OK? I know you'll be great.

I hope you enjoy having the big room to yourself. Dad said he was going to paint it for you. You even get to keep my phone. Now Joey can call you whenever he wants to. That will be okay too. You'll see.

I love you, Baby Sister. I always will. I am so proud of you. I'm still here when you need me.

I love you.

Francesca

When I finished reading that letter I was sobbing. I could never forget the pain in my heart and the smile on my face when I read it, though. Daddy heard me crying and came into my room. He sat on my bed and held me while I cried. He asked me, "What happened? *Che c'è?*"

I held up the letter just as Mom walked into the room. "*O, non mi dire. Franca…*" her voice trailed off. I nodded.

Daddy hugged me. "She is still your sister!" he reassured me.

I was unable to catch my breath as I tried to explain through my hiccups. "Ever since I was little…when Benny or my sisters…made me angry…I wished…I wished…that I…that I…was an only child. Now…now…they all left me…and I'm alone…I don't want to be alone…I want my sister!"

Daddy teased me. "You see what happens? First you want them to leave you alone. Now you miss everybody!"

Mom pointed something out to me. "*Non ti preoccupare,* no worry," she said, "*Tua sorella Pina non ci lascia mai.* Josephine will never leave us. You feel alone you go next door by your sister!" We were all laughing now.

My parents tucked me in that night for the first time in years. They each kissed me goodnight on the cheek. When they went to their room, one at a time they called out, *"Buona notte."* I smiled and called back, *"Buona notte."* Then when they closed my door and I heard theirs close as well, I turned my head to the wall and held onto my pillow. I cried for my sister that night. Things would never be the same.

Part Two

Fall, 1989

After Francesca's wedding, we all went back to our regular routines. Daddy still worked the twelve to eight o'clock shift at the hospital. I still worked at the same place, still until about nine thirty at night. Mom was not working anymore for a while by then. She was only forty-nine, but her back pain and arthritis were awful at times. Mom had started working when she was only fourteen years old, lying about her age to get a job at a tobacco company. Her task was to put the cigarettes into their packages and seal them.

Nonna Giuseppa struggled to raise her children as a widow. When Mom was still going to school, the nuns were partial to her because she had never known her father. They knew how difficult things were for Nonna Giuseppa. They would give my mother clothes and shoes to help out. Sometimes they would even give Mom cash to bring home to Nonna so she could buy food. Mom said Nonna would make a lot of different kinds of pasta because it was too expensive to buy meat. Nonna made pasta with potatoes, pasta with vegetables, pasta with garlic and oil, whatever it took to help her children forget that there was no meat on the table. As a result of this diet, Mom suffered from anemia. Zia Carmela would tease her that she would never find a husband because no man wanted such a thin woman. They wanted to touch *meat*, not *bones*. Ironically Zia Carmela wound up being the thin sister and Dad was quite pleased with the meat on his wife. Zia Carmela and Daddy would tease Mom sometimes, reminding her that she was once so skinny and had to get shots from a doctor. Mom would get annoyed with her sister and husband. But then she'd laugh with them anyway.

Mom was only sixteen when she married my father. Exactly nine months after they eloped they had Maria. Then the rest of the children came one after the other. Mom stayed home with the children, and Daddy worked. Because they could not afford to live in their own place they shared a large apartment with so many other family members. Nonna Giuseppa lived with them. Nonna Giuseppa's parents, Nonna Sara and Nonno Salvatore, lived there, and Mom's aunt and uncle, Zio Paolino and Zia Margherita, lived there with their children. Maria Rosa, Mom's cousin who came for Fran's wedding, was one of their daughters.

Amazingly, everyone that lived in this apartment had their own bedroom. One bedroom per family, kids and all. They shared the kitchen and living space. The men worked outside in construction and the women worked at home with the children. Nonna Giuseppa continued to work at that same tobacco company where Mom had worked. Her job was in the cigar division, rolling out the tobacco.

When the family came to America, Mom started working at factories that manufactured men's suits. She sat at a sewing machine several hours a day, sewing the pockets onto jackets and pants. The workers sometimes did piece work, only getting paid for what they finished. This gave the employees an incentive to work faster and harder to get more done. Mom used to come home, already exhausted from one job, only to begin her other job as a mother to four children. Then I came along.

In 1970, Mom worked until she was eight months pregnant with me. When I was born, she stayed home for the first year, but after that she had to go back to work. Nonna Giuseppa was living with Zia Carmela here in America, so at first, they took care of me. Then Maria dropped out of school and started watching me by herself. Mom's difficult life had caught up with her early. At forty-nine she already had two herniated disks in her back and arthritis in her hands and knees.

I suppose I didn't appreciate or even realize all that Mom did for the family when I was younger. How often do children stop and take notice of what their mothers do for them? When Mom would get frustrated or tired she would tell us, "Wait until you have your own family to take care of, then you will realize all that your mother does for you!" And she was right, except that I was aware of it even *before* I had a child. I realized it when I was in my twenties.

Unlike my mother, I did office work for ten years. My first job after high school was at the wedding center. First I sat at the front desk, answering the switchboard. Then little by little my manager gave me more and more responsibility, none of which hurt my back or caused arthritis.

I filed paperwork, sent bills to our clients, and did inventory in my own and other departments. Within the first couple of years I was appointed assistant manager at the front desk. Then I got involved with the accounting aspect of the business, taking responsibility for seeing that our salespeople received their commissions. I made the deposits at the bank every morning, and later on, when the company converted the entire filing and billing system from manual to electronic, I was the first one trained on the program. I then had the task of training the employees in my department on the new system. Together, my manager and I upgraded all the methods for running the front office.

It was hard mental work and because it was a retail business, the hours were long. But it was certainly less of a strain than being a seamstress working at a sewing machine all day in a hot factory.

Apart from the work, I enjoyed the social aspect of the office. I went out to dinner with my colleagues; we had picnics that my employer hosted at Shea Stadium, the big Met fan that he was. Sometimes I shopped on the avenue during my lunch or dinner breaks.

After six years of working there I moved on to a more corporate setting. I wasn't quite in Manhattan, but as close as you can get before going over the bridge. I was an executive assistant for a company in Long Island City that sold decorative fabrics and wall coverings, and worked for the creative team in the design studio. I started out as the assistant to Linda, the Vice President of Design. She was a kind and talented woman whose mother had held this title before she did.

Linda was polite and generous with me, always saying "please" and "thank you." During my first week of work, she took me out to lunch at an elegant restaurant. The very next week, she asked me to accompany her to Manhattan, where, in an effort to have me feel familiar with our company, she introduced me to the sales staff at our New York showroom.

I handled all of Linda's correspondence, typing her letters, sending faxes and inter-office memos. I copyrighted original designs for her, the print designer, and the wall covering stylist. In this job, I was encouraged to use some of my own creativity and was given the task of coming up with names for the various patterns. Sometimes I was asked for my input on the names for the collection. I was even included in helping the artists and Linda design the sets for our photo shoots. Linda always made me feel like part of the design team and did not just limit me to doing paperwork all day.

Eventually Linda left the company and I became the assistant to two vice presidents. There was Kay, the woven fabrics designer, and Lorraine, the printed fabrics designer. It was very inspiring to work for these women. They were beautiful, young, and talented, and were mothers too. They each had only one daughter, and they seemed quite content that way. They were career-oriented but at the same time dedicated to their children. Their faces lit up when they talked about their girls.

The designers did a lot of traveling, both domestically and internationally, and never forgot to bring me back a gift. There were chocolate truffles from Belgium, a lemon liqueur from Italy, even a beautiful porcelain jewelry box from Germany. It was fun speaking to our vendors in South Africa, France, and more far-flung parts of the world, like China and India. Every time one of our Northern Italian vendors called, I'd be called to the phone to translate. It was even more fun when these people came to the States and visited our office. They would hug me and kiss me on both cheeks in true European style. They too would sometimes bring me little trinkets from their countries.

Of course, everyone who visited wanted coffee, and part of my job was to bring the tray with all the paraphernalia – coffee, cups, spoons, and so on, into the conference room. Usually I'd excuse myself and just discreetly return to my desk, but occasionally I was invited to sit down at the table with these people, drink coffee, and talk business with them.

I was still a proud Italian girl from Queens, with only a high school diploma, but when I was with these business professionals I felt like I was in another world. I liked it. I reveled in the intelligent conversation. I enjoyed discussing new books that one of us had read or wanted to read. During my years at this job, it was a different kind of education.

Wherever I go, I hope to learn from people. I learn from books, newspapers or magazine articles, and only recently from the Internet. It doesn't even matter if it is only a new recipe or a new word from another language.

I always share my new knowledge with my mother. Mom has always been a terrific mother but is also my best friend. We talk about everything. I think she enjoys it when I tell her my experiences at work, and she is a great listener. She smiles as I tell her stories about things people do or say, be they funny, touching, or just interesting. When I tell Mom of one of my accomplishments, I know she will always support me and say, "Wow, Susie, that's fantastic! I'm so proud of you." I love it when she says that. I guess one of these days I should tell Mom how proud I am of *her*, of all that she's been through, and of everything she did for her family. Working outside the house and taking care of a family at home was not easy, but she did it.

By the late 1980s, Mom's only job was taking care of Daddy and me. She did our laundry and cooked for us every night. She went grocery shopping and carried all the bags up three flights of stairs. Dad and I helped with the heavy cleaning but Mom took care of the everyday chores.

* * *

I did miss Fran not being at the house at night, but I admit I enjoyed having my parents to myself. Well, almost to myself. Mom was right about one thing — Josephine was still around. She and the kids were always at our apartment instead of in their own. It was okay though, because when the kids were not there I would knock on their door to see them. My nephews were like the younger siblings I never had. I got to take care of them the way my brother and sisters had taken care of me.

As time went by, Mom and I were getting more and more concerned about Daddy. We hoped those headaches had been caused by the stress of the wedding. Now it was over and had been a success. People were still calling to tell us what a beautiful wedding it was. But the headaches stuck around. They actually became more frequent and more painful. Mom started nagging Daddy again about seeing a doctor. For goodness sake, he worked at a hospital! He was buddies with many of the doctors there. He was actually very friendly with most of the staff. Everyone loved Dad at that hospital.

Every night Dad had a story from work to share with Mom and me. We knew about whose kids were getting married, which of his friends became grandparents. The younger employees went to Dad with their dating problems. I just loved it when he would tell us how one of the young people had moved in with a boyfriend or girlfriend. "What can you do?" he would comment. "That's the new style. The new generation." New style, new generation, my ass. If one of *his* kids did that he would have had a heart attack right there on the spot. Apparently he was very modern outside of his own family.

Around the family most people called Dad Battista, his middle name. But when Dad became an American citizen, his name *Giovan Battista* was changed to John, and that is what his friends and co-workers at the hospital called him. Dad's job was in housekeeping. He worked physically hard every day. You would never know it if you saw him leave the house in the morning. Dad wore a uniform at work — heavy dark blue trousers and a light blue collared shirt with a name tag on it. Only that's not how he left our apartment in the morning. Daddy rode the M train every day like an executive. He wore nice slacks, matching socks, a dress shirt, and dress shoes. All that was missing was the tie and a briefcase. He even wore a suit jacket when the weather was cool enough. You would never guess he was on his way to mop floors and take out the garbage.

Mom and I noticed that Dad's job was taking a toll on him. His previous job, in the dietary department, was much easier and more enjoyable. Then the hospital had financial trouble in the mid to late 1980s and for a while, Dad had to take a cut in hours. Then his only option was to get laid off or switch to housekeeping.

My father had loved his job in dietary. One of his duties was bringing meals to the patients. When someone he knew was in the hospital Dad took special care of them. He would use his own money to bring them a newspaper or a special treat from the cafeteria. He would lecture the patients, encouraging them to listen to their doctors so they could feel better. Only he never followed his own advice. He would not even go to see a doctor, that is, until he had no choice.

* * *

October, 1989

A normal weekend at our house always included a visit from Zia

Adriana and Zio Filippo. They'd come over for dinner and to play Five Hundred Rummy with my parents. They never left until at least three or four o'clock in the morning. Mom and Dad did not drive so it was easier for Mr. and Mrs. C, as Dad called them, to come to our house. Daddy was referring to the *Happy Days* characters, Mr. and Mrs. Cunningham, whom Fonzie and Richie's friends called Mr. and Mrs. C. Dad was being funny and the reference kind of stuck.

Dad also preferred having company at home instead of going out. His friends knew how he was and did not seem to mind. I am sure that Mom would have enjoyed getting out more often but still, she liked having company.

I loved it when Zia Adriana and Zio Filippo came over. First of all, it was like a live comedy show. Daddy and Zio would drink their wine or some other drink, Mom and Zia yelling at them. Their visit also gave me my big chance to stay out a little past curfew. I was a year out of high school but was still expected to be home by eleven o'clock or midnight. Only on special occasions was I allowed to stay out any later than that. But when my aunt and uncle were over, Daddy was happy and preoccupied and he'd forget to check his watch when I came in the door. He would not be watching for me with his head out the bedroom window either.

When I came home those nights, I'd stay up with them as they played cards. They would play at the dining room table and I would enjoy the show from the couch. I would not even turn the television on, I got such a kick out of hearing them laugh and argue. Of course I would always side with Zio Filippo and Daddy. "Oh leave them alone!" I would yell out from the couch. I loved to join in. "Let them have fun!"

Zio Filippo got bolder when I stuck up for them. "You see, Susie? You tell them. We are having a good time. Who cares?"

I was not around one night when their fun was interrupted. The four of them were about to start playing when Dad dropped his cards and went to sit in his chair. He held his head with both hands as the color drained from his face. The other three rose up quickly from their seats and rushed to his side. "What happened, Battista?" *Che hai?*" Mom was frightened.

"*La testa sempra che mi sta scopiare, Silvana!*" was Dad's way of expressing to Mom that his head felt like it was about to explode.

Now Mommy was angry. "That's it! *BASTA!* You are going to the doctor or else we are going to fight!!!"

Zia Adriana tried to calm them both down. "You said after Franca's wedding. That's it now, Battista. Is it just a bad headache you feel or other things too? *Cos'è che ti senti?* What is it you feel?"

Dad finally confided in his friends and his wife. "It's not just my head. It's my eyes. I thought maybe I needed new glasses. I paid a lot of money but they didn't help me. My eyes, my legs too. Even my legs now. They get so tired. The stairs never used to bother me before. I always came straight up the stairs. Now I climb up one flight of the stairs and I need to rest. The next flight I do the same thing. *No non posso stare.* I can't stay like this. This week I go to the doctor. I have to."

As she let out a deep breath Mom cried out, "*Finalmente!*" It's about time.

That week Daddy kept his word and he and Mom went to see a doctor. The doctor gave Daddy a complete physical, including some X-rays. After not being satisfied with those tests, the doctor wanted to take more tests. He knew he had to admit Dad into the hospital the very next day.

All Mom and Daddy told me was that Dad had a bad case of bronchitis and had to go to the hospital. Mom tells me now how she did tell me then about the doctor's concerns but I do not remember that. Who knows? Maybe she told everyone but me. Maybe my memory blocked it out because it was too difficult to take seriously. I just remember Mom looking so upset. As usual,

Dad and I teased her and made some jokes. Mom would barely crack a smile and then just leave the room.

And so the next day Dad was admitted into the same hospital where he worked. His friends were in and out of his room, bringing him the Italian newspaper that he always read every day. He found extra treats on his food trays when his meals were delivered. The friends stopped in during their lunch hours and before leaving work for the evening. They treated Daddy like a king and the rest of us like his royal family.

Daddy's doctor ran a whole series of tests while Dad was in the hospital. He even sent Dad by ambulance to another location for a CT scan of his brain. Well, the CT scan solved the mystery of Dad's headaches. It revealed a brain tumor.

I got the news when Mom called me at work and told me to come straight home when I finished for the day. When I walked into the apartment my heart sank. Everyone was already there. My sisters and my brother were there. *They* rarely came over during the week. Zia Adriana and Zio Filippo were there, along with Mom's sisters, Zia Maria and Zia Carmela. Zia Rosaria of course was in Florida. Even some of my cousins were over. I knew it was not a party. Something was terribly wrong. It had to be Daddy.

I was not there when they told Mom about the tumor. My brother Benny had called the doctor earlier that day to get an update on the results of all these tests they had run on Dad. Benny was the first to know about the tumor. Then he called my sisters. But no one told me. I was still the baby to them so I was always the last to know anything. It was Ben's idea to call Zia Adriana and Mom's sisters. He wanted them there when he broke the news to Mommy. He was not sure how she would react.

When Mom came home from the hospital, everyone but me was already at our house. I found out later that night from Francesca what Mom's reaction was when she walked into a house full of people with somber faces. Apparently, she became agitated right away. It was obvious that her sisters and Zia Adriana had been crying.

"What is it?" Mom demanded *"Che sta sucedendo?"* she asked, needing to know what happened. Benny led her by the hand to a chair and made her sit down as he explained what the doctor had told him. When he finished speaking, Mom sat there, numb. My aunts got nervous and tried to get her to let out her emotions.

"Cry," they told her. "It's okay *se vuoi piangere, qui siamo* Silvana," assuring her that she was not alone. "We're here, Silvana. *"Non sei sola."* Still, Mom was numb. *"Non ti preoccupare che l'auitano,"* they continued all at once, telling Mom that the doctors were on the case. "He's going to be okay," they reassured her. They lied.

I do not remember who told me the news or how they did. I just remember feeling nauseous. Nauseous and terrified. The only reason I did not throw up or cry was that I did not want to make my mother more upset than she already was. Then I recall a bunch of us sitting around the kitchen table. I went behind my mother's chair and put my arms around her. I kissed her gently on the cheek and squeezed her. She smiled slightly and patted my hand.

"Don't worry, Mommy," I said, "He'll be okay. Hey, I still have to get married! Dad has to give me away. Remember what we planned for the party? Hamburgers and French fries for dinner. Ice cream instead of a big fat wedding cake. Daddy would not miss that!" I was smiling for my mother's sake, although my heart was aching.

Everyone laughed except for Mom. She buried her face in her hands and finally started to cry. My cousin Lisa scolded me. "Wrong thing to say, Sue," as she came over to put her arms around me.

"I know," I sobbed. "I'm sorry. I am trying to think positive before I go crazy!"

My mother prayed in between breaths. *"O, Dio Mio*, Oh, God. He still has this daughter. His baby. Let him live, please, to see her get married!"

Now everyone was weeping and wiping tears from their faces. No one dared to move or speak. *This cannot be real*, I thought. Only it was. The part about burgers and ice cream was a joke between my father and me because we could not believe how expensive it was to have a wedding. We had joked about it as we planned Francesca's wedding. I had said, "This much for a cake! Damn!! I will get an ice cream cake when I get married."

My father would add, "Okay, good. Then we could have French fries and hamburgers for the dinner. Instead of limousines we could ride bicycles to the church."

Only one problem with that is that I did not own a bicycle. I was never allowed to have one. Daddy did not want me to get hurt on a bike. He did not want me to skin my knees or break an arm cycling along the concrete sidewalks. He would not even buy me roller skates because he thought they were dangerous, too. The only reason I had a pair of skates is that I received them as a gift.

My cousin and I were in the same sixth grade class. My grades were good and she was not doing so well. Our teacher suggested we work together after school. Her mom gave me the roller skates for Christmas as a thank you gift for helping her daughter. My cousin got to be Student of the Month for improving her grades and I got my roller skates. Dad would watch me from the window every time I went outside to skate. I was only allowed to skate in front of the house and never in the street.

Mom would get angry when we mentioned our burgers and ice cream wedding plan. "Sure! *Padre e figlia* figured it out already!" And Dad and I would rub it in even more. It was a special little joke between us, and we enjoyed it.

The next day the doctor explained to Mom and Dad about the tumor. He recommended a surgeon at a specialized cancer hospital in Manhattan. He gave Mom a copy of the test results and set up an appointment with the oncologist. My mother went there with Zia

Adriana. The doctor pointed out the tumor in the films and explained that it was the size of an egg and needed to be removed immediately. I do not know how doctors can tell this from the initial testing, but he also added that the tumor was most likely malignant, so they would be running more tests while Dad was there in the hospital. It must have been terrifying for my mother to learn that there was a strong chance it was cancer and that it may have already spread or even originated in another part of the body. That would be revealed after the surgery.

My mother now was nauseous. She felt so weak and sick that the doctor had to explain the details to Zia Adriana. Thank God *she* was there. Later, Zia Adriana explained everything to my brother and sisters. Again, all they told me was that Dad needed surgery to remove a brain tumor. They said nothing about it most likely being cancer. My friend's husband had a brain tumor removed several years before that and he was fine now. So I had hope. Besides, this was my father. He *had* to be okay.

* * *

November, 1989

Dad was transferred to another hospital the first week of November. The night before his surgery I could not sleep. Too many thoughts went through my head. *How could this be happening?* Daddy was never even sick and never complained about his health. Even with the headaches, he had never verbalized the pain until that one night. We only realized his discomfort from his face.

I was so nervous, so frightened. Then of course I thought about Mom and wondered how she must be feeling. My parents had known each other since Mom was seven years old. Mom's Nonna Sara lived next door to Daddy's family. As a young man, Daddy stayed out late against Nonna Maria's wishes. Nonna Maria would lock him out of the house to teach him a lesson. Sara would leave her door open on purpose. Daddy would climb over their adjoining balcony and sleep over at Nonna Sara's house.

Eventually, Dad and Zio Rocco, Mom's brother, worked together and became friends. Daddy would often tell me of the first time he noticed my mother as a grown woman. It is one of my favorite stories.

"One day after work, Zio Rocco and I walked home together. As we got closer to his mother's house, he invited me in for coffee. 'Okay,' I told him. 'Thank you, *Grazie*.' When we got inside only your mother was home. So Zio Rocco, he told Mommy, 'Go make coffee for me and Battista.' So I smile at Mommy and she smiled too. She went and made the coffee. When she finished, Zio Rocco and I sat at the table. Mommy came over and she served us." His eyes sparkled as he thought back to that day. "Your mother," he would say, "had on a long dress that reached her ankles. It was tight up to here (as he motioned to his waist) with a belt. On top she had three or four buttons and the first button was open. The bottom was loose over her legs. Her hair was long and wavy. It was the color of chestnuts. Then she bent down just a little to pour the coffee. I saw just a little bit of her breasts. Just a little." Then his face would turn bright red as he let out a loud laugh. "I got a little curious. Then I caught myself that I was looking too much so I turned my face. I didn't want Zio Rocco to punch me. He used to be a boxer, you know!" He would laugh again. "*Buon anima*, he was strong *tuo zio*! Then it's not right. He was my friend and I was looking at his sister that way. His baby sister. He would be right if he punched me! For me that day I saw the most beautiful woman, your mother."

Mom was always so embarrassed by that story. I think it's priceless.

Mom's brother Zio Rocco died in 1975. Two months before his forty-fifth birthday he went into the hospital with pneumonia and never came home. He left behind his wife and four sons. Zia had to raise four sons by herself in 1970s Brooklyn, and that was no easy task. Over the years, their sons moved out of New York and all have families and lives of their own now. With the grace of God they all survived the more difficult years following their father's death.

Enzo and Orazio (who is named for our grandfather) live close to one another in Europe. Rodolfo lives in Texas, where he owns and operates a thriving business that carries the family name. Zio Rocco must be smiling with pride because of that. And Valentino, the youngest of Zio's sons, lives with his family in Florida, with the majority of our relatives.

Did you notice his third and fourth sons' names, Rodolfo and Valentino? Zia had chosen the name Rodolfo when the first baby was born, so when she was in labor with the next child, Zio Rocco told my mother, "This is Valentino coming."

My mother turned to Zio and asked him, "How do you know that's Valentino? You don't know. What if it's a girl?"

Zio Rocco shook his head, "No, my wife named Rodolfo. Now this one is Valentino. I know it already."

My mother and Nonna Giuseppa were in the bedroom assisting Zia as she was giving birth. When the infant was born and the women realized it was a boy, Mom was crying tears of joy for her new nephew. "Valentino!" she cried out. "Valentino!" My mother had thought Zio Rocco was just being smug, but he was right after all.

The two brothers were named for the infamous Rudolph Valentino, whom the females pined over in those days. And I can tell you that these two men are just as handsome. (Not just because they're my cousins, either!)

Zia is still living in Brooklyn. Recently, she was very ill and in the hospital so I got to see three of her four sons. It is so sweet the way my cousins still squeeze my cheeks and lovingly kiss my face when they see me. They still think of me as a baby because we were apart so much of the time I was growing up. Zio's eldest son, Enzo, calls me, "la mia bambolina," which means "my little doll." It's good for my self-esteem, being called "a little doll" at thirty-something years old.

Enzo, Rudy, and Valentino, are grandfathers now, while Orazio's five children are still very young. Mom and Zia still speak on the telephone a few times a month, and occasionally they get together. Recently, the two sisters-in-law shared Easter dinner together at Mom's house. I went to visit with them for a little while before I went on with my own plans for the holiday. It was interesting to hear the two women reminisce about the past. That is when I heard the story of how my cousins got their names.

When Zio died, Mom took it so badly. He was the person in her life who was the closest to a father figure. When Mom was a little girl and the school children would make cards for their fathers, Mom would make a card for Zio Rocco. Too bashful to give it to him herself, she would place it beside his dinner dish. The untimely, early loss of her brother was another heartache in my mother's life.

In the midst of my nostalgic moment I must have fallen asleep. Hours later I jumped out of bed. I heard voices, sirens, and footsteps all over the building. Then I heard a neighbor's voice in the hallway. "What happened?" he asked. "What's going on?"

A detective answered him. "Well Sir, a man has jumped off the roof of this building. Please go back into your apartment so the officers can do their job. Thank you, Sir."

I panicked. *Oh, my God! Oh no, did Daddy sneak out of the hospital? Did he come home last night and jump off the roof? No it can't be! He would never, would he?* I ran to my bedroom window and picked up the blinds. *Oh no! Please God, no!* There was a man's body on the cement floor in the backyard. From my bedroom window all I could see were the man's legs and feet. I could not see his upper body or his face. He was wearing the same blue pants Daddy wore for work. On his feet were the same heavy black shoes Daddy wore with his uniform. *Please God, please God, no!*

I made the sign of the cross and raced inside to the kitchen window. Someone was knocking on the door but I ignored it. Mom was up and she unlocked the door. My heart was racing. *Was that man, was he, my father?*

Before I could open the window Josephine's husband Jack grabbed me and turned me around. "Sue, come on, calm down, please calm down," he told me.

"Oh, God, tell me the truth! Is it Daddy? I couldn't see the man's face. Tell me, please!" I screamed. Jack pulled me into his arms and tried to calm me down.

"No, kid, I promise. Dad is in the hospital. In the city, safe and sound. He's okay, Sue, he's okay," he reassured me. Suddenly I just tensed up. I could no longer speak. Jack led me to Dad's chair and made me sit down. He went over to the top of a wooden cabinet where the liquor bottles were kept and grabbed a bottle. He got a glass with ice from the kitchen and filled it with scotch. "Drink this," he said, "it will calm your nerves a little bit." I drank down half the glass in one gulp.

Just then there was another knock at the door. It was the same detective I heard earlier in the hallway. "We are asking all of the tenants if they heard anything, anything unusual last night or even early this morning." I was shaking as I answered, finding my voice once more. The ice in my glass was rattling. Mom took the glass out of my hand.

"My father is sick!" I said. "He is in the hospital! Today is his brain surgery!" That is all I could say before my vocal cords went numb.

Now Mom was crying too. "Who was it?" she questioned. "Do you know yet?"

Still writing in a notebook the detective answered, "Downstairs. Third floor apartment."

Mom cried out, "Oh, poor man, that poor man!"

I was such a mess that morning and could not calm down. I was grateful Dad was safe and sound at the hospital but I was sad it was someone I knew. A nice old man I said hello to each day on the stoop or in the hallway. Sad for his family. The sadness consumed me that morning. I could barely get dressed and ready to go out. I knew there was nothing I could do at the hospital but I had to be there. I needed to be with my family. We all needed to be there together.

It was the longest day I have ever known. The surgery on Dad's brain lasted seven hours. We all sat there so quietly. I imagine everyone was doing exactly what I was. Praying, in my mind, over and over again. I said every prayer I could remember from eight years of Catholic school. Ironically outside of this well known cancer hospital so many people were smoking cartons' worth of cigarettes, my brother and sisters included. While they were outside, I sat beside Mom and held onto her arm. She was so quiet, barely moving. Poor Mom. One year earlier she had watched Nonna Giuseppa die.

It was Mom's turn to stay overnight, now in a different hospital praying for her husband to live with every ounce of faith she had. I tried reading a book, but could not concentrate. Some man loved some woman, that's all I remember about the story. I ate some chocolate, my vice. I looked at the clock a thousand times. Then I glanced at my brother biting his nails. Maria biting her lip. Josephine was rubbing her pregnant belly. Fran had her legs crossed and was rocking back and forth on a chair, a childhood habit she never grew out of. Time was dragging and dragging.

Just when I thought time had stopped completely the doctor appeared. We all stood up at the same exact moment. The doctor went right to Mom. Maria's husband Joe stood beside her on one side. Benny stood on the other side. "The surgery went well," he began. "We did remove the tumor from his brain but he will still need radiation treatment. We will make him as comfortable as possible. From what we have learned today however, chances are he will not survive another year."

A PUNCH IN THE GUT!!! A hard one. That bad cramp and nausea you feel right before diarrhea. Damn it! God knows what all the words were that came out of the doctor's mouth. That is what my brain recalls. Once I heard "won't survive another year," everything went into slow motion. I saw people's mouths moving, all of us turning around in different directions and all of us crying hysterically. The person whose reaction left an impression on me the most was Maria's husband Joe G. We call him that because there are so many Joes and Josephines in the family. Joe G. is usually calm and level headed. He is usually the one who can take charge. He keeps other people calm when something upsetting happens. But this time he lost it and was crying like the rest of us. He was cursing. His arms were flying around, probably searching for something to hit. I never saw him that way and have never seen him like that since.

What a disaster! Our lives were crumbling before us. *Daddy, don't leave us. Please!* That's all I could think. *It's not real, it can't be!*

Once we all calmed down we began another waiting period. We waited for Dad to leave the recovery room and be brought to his own room. As the others went to smoke again, I sat and thought of Joe G. As destroyed as I was for myself, I felt as bad for him. His pain made me feel even worse. He and Dad had a special relationship that was created by the efforts of many people.

Joe G. came to our family in 1976 when my cousin Yolanda was dating a man named Dominick. Yola and Maria were close. Dominick had a good friend named Joe. Together Yola and Dominick arranged a blind date for Maria and Joe G. to meet. Dad had no idea. After two dates Joe wanted to see more of Maria and vice versa. So Maria explained how she was not allowed out very often, even though she was nineteen years old. Joe told Maria he wanted to meet her father and ask his permission to date her. Maria was terrified.

Maria was Mom and Dad's first baby, but age had nothing to do with anything. Mom and Dad were so young when they had Maria. Not only was she their daughter but a friend to them as well, their right arm. And she was like a third parent to the rest of us kids.

As the big sister, Maria had to open doors for the rest of us. So it was Maria who would have to get Daddy to soften up enough to allow a stranger into our home. A man who could one day become an in-law. Joe too, would lay the groundwork for whomever the rest of us brought home some day.

Dad refused to meet Joe, that is, until he did some investigating. He wanted details. Who was this man who wanted his daughter? How did they meet? Where was he from? Who were his parents? How old was he? Did he have a job? The list went on. It turned out Dad knew an uncle of Joe's because they once worked together. Luckily, Dad respected Joe's uncle and trusted his opinion.

Joe's uncle reassured Dad about Joe. He spoke very highly of him, saying he was a good man, very respectful to his family. He always worked and was very responsible. He urged Daddy to give his nephew a chance and said he was confident Dad would be happy. Still, though, Daddy was very stubborn. Mom had to practically *beg* him on Maria's behalf.

Finally the day arrived when Joe came alone to meet Daddy for the first time. I wish I knew what that conversation was like. Joe and Maria still could not go out alone. Joe was only allowed to visit Maria in the apartment when Dad was at home.

After a couple of months of this, Joe's parents came over to meet our family. I was too young to remember what that was like, although I do know that Joe's family and ours have always respected each other.

One of Joe's cousins got Maria a job at the sweater factory where she herself worked. Joe was allowed to drive Maria back and forth to work when he was not working overtime. Soon Maria was permitted to visit Joe's house or one of his relative's houses, with conditions of course. Joe's parents had to be present at all times and Maria had to take one of her siblings along. Usually it was me.

I was Maria's baby from the moment I was born. I was five and a half years old when Maria and Joe began dating. They took me everywhere with them. We would visit Joe's relatives or friends. We would go out for ice cream or take rides in Joe's red Fiat. I remember one time we took a boat ride on Sheepshead Bay. The two of them would hold my hand when we walked together and sometimes when Joe was over at the apartment, I would sit between them on the couch. I would often go with Maria to Joe's parents' house, too.

Joe's family watched me grow up. Despite having to share Maria's attention, I loved Joe quickly. It did not take long for Mom and Dad to become fond of Joe too. He had earned Daddy's trust by always bringing Maria home at the time Daddy had told him to. He was very thoughtful and sociable with our relatives, and enjoyed a mutual respect with Daddy. And so in 1977, Joe and Maria were engaged. Less than a year after that, they were married, but I cannot recall when Joe G. was not part of this family.

As the first son-in-law in our family, Joe became a close friend to Daddy. Like Dad, Joe was born in Sicily, and the two of them shared similar values and traditions. I guess that's why it was not such a big deal to Joe that Daddy was so strict. An only son himself, he felt just as protective of his sisters. Over the years, Joe and Dad became more like a father and a son, and certainly meant a lot to each other. Joe felt the punch of Daddy's prognosis as hard as the rest of us did, and in the months to follow Joe proved more than ever that his uncle had been right about him.

Several hours had passed before Daddy was brought to his room. The doctors only gave us a moment to see him before we left. Daddy was still groggy when I saw him. His head was bandaged and he was lying flat on the bed. His eyes, how I can still visualize them. Those strong, intense eyes. They looked wildly at me as if Daddy were straining to see me. Still calm, he patted my hand and touched my cheek. "Okay, *Gioia*, go home with your sister. It's okay."

My lips quivered. "Okay, *Papà*, I'm okay. You rest now. I love you, Daddy."

He squeezed my hand, barely looking at me. "I love you too, Sweetheart. It's okay, Baby, *Papà sta bene,*" he said, so that I would know, or at least *think* he was okay. Another lie.

I walked out of his room with tears on my face. As we left the hospital I held on to Josephine as if I had to protect her and the baby in her belly. We held hands the whole ride back to Queens. Mom stayed at the hospital. She watched Daddy all night from a chair beside his bed. The pain in her back, shooting up her spine. There was no time for that now. A nurse brought her something to eat and some kind of pill for her back pain.

When we got home, Josephine would not leave me alone in the apartment. She slept with Jason, who was just three and a half years old, in our parents' bed. David and Michael, now nine and seven years old, slept in my old room. I sat for hours rocking in Daddy's chair. I was getting used to not sleeping. I just sat there in a daze. My eyes were burning and my face was wet with tears. *What the hell is going on? This is not right! This is not fair!* Everyone else was married. I was all grown up and could take care of myself. This was supposed to be my parents' time together. Now look at them. Daddy in a hospital, fighting for his life! Damn it! It wasn't fair. I was about to grow up really fast. It scared me.

The past summer was now a distant memory. So much had changed already. The weeks after Daddy's first surgery were a nightmare. While he was recovering in the hospital they kept running tests on the rest of his body. The tests revealed that Dad also had lung cancer. Once he was strong enough he had more surgery. The doctors removed one quarter of his lung.

This all seemed unreal to me. Overwhelming. I worked long hours and if I had a day or night off, I went to see Daddy at the hospital. Mom practically lived there with him. I barely recognized my home anymore. As it had once been so full, now it was always empty.

Thanksgiving was coming and Daddy insisted we all celebrate the holiday. He would not be home but everyone had in-laws to go to.

Everyone except me, that is. Mom would be staying at the hospital of course, but Daddy did not want me to spend the holiday feeling bad. Fat chance. Everyone invited me to go wherever they were going but I did not want to. I would have spent the day with my Joey but he was in Sicily. His grandmother was very ill that year and Joey's mother insisted the whole family go together. They did not know if she would be around the following year.

I decided I did not feel like being thankful. I was losing my father and there was nothing I could do about it. No, I was not going anywhere. I was staying home, in *my* home, all by myself. That was the plan.

On Thanksgiving Day I woke up, showered, and put my pajamas back on. I had picked up a frozen turkey dinner the night before. There was a pumpkin pie and whipped cream in the fridge which Fran had dropped off in the morning. Dad and I were the only ones who liked pumpkin pie and Fran always bought it for us. She wanted me to have the pie for me and for Daddy and I was happy to oblige. And I thought it only right to also have a glass of wine, too, on Dad's behalf. He could not drink these days, what with all the medication he was taking and still being in the hospital. I went through the cabinets and kissed a bottle of red wine that I found. Well, the day was looking up. I would have a glass of wine with my dinner and another glass for dessert. Daddy loved to eat apples that were cored and cut up that soaked in the wine. You eat the wine-drenched apples, then you drink. It's quite delicious. In the summer you could have peaches with white wine.

Thinking about the apples and wine reminded me of Sunday dinners at our house, the way they were before Daddy got sick. Especially the ones when I was little. I had never realized how special those dinners were. At that time, Daddy would let me eat the apples but he would have to drink the wine that was left in the glass. It was our special dessert. And the dinner that came before dessert was just as delicious.

As Daddy got older he enjoyed cooking the Sunday dinner. He woke up early and made coffee. He always brought a cup to Mommy in their bedroom. Then he would go back into the kitchen and get the meal started. Mom would join him and clean up after him as he cooked. Together they made the best meat sauce I ever tasted. It was full of chopped meat and had big chunks of stew meat. There were also beef bones and pigs' feet. Sometimes they added potatoes, sometimes peas. Mom had to use a slotted spoon to make my plate because I hated the peas. Now I never make meat sauce without them. My favorite part of the sauce was the meatballs. I liked them fried before they were put in the sauce. Sometimes I even ate them for breakfast.

Fran and I were awakened many times by a meatball breakfast. I would smell them even before I got out of bed. As soon as the meatballs were fried, Dad brought them to our room. One plate, two meatballs, and two forks. "Good Morning my sweethearts, time to wake up!" That was our Sunday morning greeting. Fran would put her pillow over her head, choosing sleep over food. I would jump down from the top bunk and follow Daddy and the meatballs into the kitchen. I usually ate my meatball and Fran's too.

Every Sunday was like a holiday. The married people came over too. We sat around that table, ready for a feast. Mom would have olives and cheese on the table as the pasta cooked. There was always plenty of Italian bread for dipping into the sauce. We all started out with a plate of pasta. The girls would then get up to clear the pasta dishes and bring bowls of meat to the table. There was always a big bowl of salad to accompany the meat. After eating and conversation, the meat dishes were cleared and the fruit was brought to the table. That's when Dad would let me sample his wine and apples. Occasionally Mom would catch him passing me his glass and slap his arm. "*Basta!*" she'd scold. That's enough. Dad would pull the glass away from me until Mom got back to the kitchen. Daddy and I would laugh as he passed the glass back over to me and I took a sip of the wine. Since Dad liked to watch westerns he was also a fan of *John Wayne*. So his nickname became *John Wine*, but only within the family. Coffee and pastries came later on. First the women washed the dishes and cleared the table while the guys napped or watched television.

After Sunday dinner Dad would disappear into Benny's bedroom. I always knew where he was headed and followed him. I would peek at him from the doorway and smile. Daddy would pretend to be surprised. Then he would wink at me and would whisper, "Good night, see you later." I would go to my room and wait. As soon as I heard Daddy snoring I put my shoes on and headed outside to play. His naps never lasted very long.

It was much easier to get Mom's permission to go outside while Daddy was asleep, instead of taking the chance that he would say no. Soon after my escape, I would look up and see him smiling out the window as he blew out the cigarette smoke from his mouth. He would watch me from the window and look away each time I looked up. Once it got dark he would not yell out my name. He would whistle. That distinctive whistle with two-fingers-in-his-mouth father whistle. I'd look up at him and with his hand he would motion that it was time to go upstairs. If I tried to argue I got "the eyes" and the two fingers across the neck motion. No negotiating allowed.

I laughed through my tears as I remembered those days. I was suddenly missing my family and then, as if God had read my thoughts, the telephone rang. It was Josephine. "Hey sister!" she said, half laughing.

"Hey Jo, what's up?" I heard voices yelling out and my sister laughed, "Okay, okay, relax!" she called out to them. Then she let me in on what was happening. She and her family were at Jack's parents' house. The whole family was there. Jack's father had asked what our family was doing for the holiday, since Dad was in the hospital. He was so pissed off at Josephine for letting me stay home alone. Then with a slammed fist on the table he insisted, "No one eats dinner until Aunt Sue gets here! Go call your sister or nobody eats!" That's why Josephine was laughing and everyone else was laughing in the background.

As Josephine was telling me what happened, I heard her father-in-law's voice. Josephine held the phone to him and Gene yelled in my ear. "Hurry up there, Aunt Sue. Everyone's hungry. Get your ass in a cab and get over here. We'll wait outside and pay the driver." I laughed as I suddenly realized I was still in my pajamas.

So I would not be alone after all. Jack's family, like Joe G.'s family, had watched me grow up. I called Jack's parents *Poppa Gene* and *Aunt Joanie*. Jack's whole family called me *Aunt Sue* because I was only nine and a half years old when David was born. As a kid I would cry when Josephine went to their house without me. I loved the attention they gave me, calling me *Aunt Sue*, like a grown up.

When I got to their house that day, we ate dinner immediately. Everyone was starving, thanks to me. They all teased me about it at the dinner table. Poppa Gene was cursing at Josephine and Jack for leaving me home in the first place. I ate my pumpkin pie and whipped cream in company. I brought some part of being Italian to the table with my red wine too. Thanksgiving turned out to be a good day for me after all. Thanks to Poppa Gene, a tough little Irishman from Brooklyn. I was grateful.

At the hospital, Mom and Dad were not alone either. My godmother, Zia Maria, had gone with Mom in the morning to spend the day there. Zia Maria's kids had also moved to Florida by then. She and my godfather, Zio Achille, were separated for many years. Zia lived in an apartment a few blocks away from us. Zio Achille moved around a lot. But despite their separation, I was always close to both of my godparents. They loved me so much and I adored them. My godfather would often live far away so I did not see him very often growing up. Mom would always remind me to send a card for his birthday. Once, when he lived in the Bronx, I sent him a card and enclosed a poem I wrote especially for him. When I went to visit him I saw that he had it hung up on the wall where he worked.

Zio Achille was a baker and he was so good at it. When he explained to his friends who I was, they told me, "So *you* are the godchild he brags about! He reads that card every day and smiles!" Shyly, I hugged my godfather and hid my face in his chest. He kissed the top of my head and squeezed me tightly. I love to watch the 8mm films of my first birthday, in which I am in my godfather's arms as he points to my cake. He had baked it himself. On top of the cake sits a beautiful carousel with a red and white canopy. Seeing Zio Achille was always a treat for me.

Zia Maria always lived near us. At one point in my childhood we lived on the same block. Not just my family and Zia Maria. Her daughters Josephine, Sylvia, and Carmen lived on the same block too. Her son Frankie was still single and living at home at the time. My cousins, who were much older than I, had kids my age or even older. I went to Catholic School because their kids went to Catholic School.

My mother and her nieces worked, so that left Zia Maria with the big job of taking the kids back and forth to school. All of us. Our school was about thirteen blocks away from where we lived. We walked to school and back home again every day. Zia Maria and eight children. In age order, we were Maria, Joey, Tony, Lisa, Angela, Me, Steven, and Tara.

I did not start school until I was six years old. The principal wanted to start me in kindergarten. Zia Maria refused. "No, she is six years old she go to the first grade!" When the principal argued the importance of kindergarten, Zia Maria would not give up. "Not my godchild! She no need the kindergarten. She knows her numbers and letters already. I show you. You give her a test, then you understand." The principal was frazzled and did just that. I was given an assessment test and passed with flying colors. So first grade it was. I skipped kindergarten because my godmother believed in me. And because she had a hard head.

Our first year at the school there was no lunchroom. The parents had to come and pick up their children for lunch and bring them back every afternoon. Zia Maria put her boxing gloves on once more and got ready for the battle. She called and yelled and bothered the principal so much until she had the school make room for the children to eat lunch. She was famous among the teachers and parents that year.

Mom and Daddy were so glad to have Zia Maria with them. She was the oldest of Mom's sisters and wanted to be treated accordingly. Daddy would tease her on purpose and she could not help but laugh when he did that. She'd let out a loud laugh, smiling from ear to ear with her big red lips. Age did not matter; she always wore the reddest lipstick she could find and the reddest nail polish to match. Mom's sisters loved Daddy, and so did the nieces and nephews. Even the second cousins loved him.

Zio Battista, as they called Dad, loved making them laugh. At family parties he always left the adults for at least a little while. He would come in to check on us kids. He would come in all serious and say, "Okay, now you are all in trouble! Everybody cry!" We would all rub our eyes and fall over, pretending we were crying. Daddy would be laughing so hard clutching his chest. "Okay, shut up, stop! Everybody now laugh!" We all would scream out and laugh so hard we could not stop. One of the other adults would usually come in to see what all the commotion was about. My cousins still talk about that.

Mom, Dad, and Zia Maria talked about the old days. Zia Maria and Zio Achille were considering moving back in together. Daddy was trying to convince Zia to do that because he did not want his sister-in-law to be alone the rest of her life. "He is still your husband," he told her. "You are alone. He is alone. You could be company for one another." As always, Zia was being stubborn. But eventually, they actually did get back together. Counseling Zia Maria and making her laugh was a good distraction for Daddy.

As Daddy spoke to Zia Maria that Thanksgiving Day, the food arrived. Our cousin Sebastiano, who was a chef at a New York restaurant, prepared four Thanksgiving meals and drove them over to the hospital. He pulled up a chair and the four of them reminisced about the old days. Talking about the 1970s in Brooklyn. The days in Tripoli when Sebastiano was just a boy living with Mom and Dad and his own family. He was one of Zia Margherita and Zio Paolino's sons. That was the family that shared the apartment in Tripoli with Mom and Dad. Sebastiano's family had moved back to Italy and Sebastiano made his way to The United States, where he fell in love with Angela, one of Zia Maria's daughters. Sebastiano and Angela got married and had three great kids together, two girls and a boy. Sebastiano's wife and children were living in Florida by then but he was making better money as a chef in Manhattan, so he stayed in New York and spent long weekends in Florida with his family. He too was grateful for the company.

Daddy and Sebastiano discussed their days in Tripoli. The men going out to work each morning, the women with their hands full at home. Because they did not have a refrigerator they had to go to market and buy only what they would prepare for each day. They did laundry outside with a washboard and basin. They pressed clothes with a hot coal iron. Air conditioning was unheard of. The women mopped the tile floors each day with cold water to ease some of the heat. Daddy had an ally now, having Sebastiano at the hospital with him. The two of them had fun together teasing the women. They told dirty jokes to annoy them and the women pretended to be offended. The four of them had their own little Thanksgiving right there in Daddy's room. Despite their fatigue, Mom and Dad had a special day with their sister and cousin. It was just what they needed.

Dad's stay in the hospital that fall lasted thirty-two days. The doctor arranged it so Daddy could have radiation treatments after the holidays. He needed time to recover and regain his strength after two major surgeries. In the meantime, we were ready to celebrate. Celebrate Daddy coming home and celebrate the upcoming holidays. In our hearts we knew it would be our last Christmas with Daddy. It had to be the best one we ever had.

***

December, 1989 - The Homecoming

Dad came home the first week of December. Once again our home was full of people. My sisters and brothers-in-law were there. Zia Adriana and Zio Filippo were there. Maria's father-in-law came over. My cousins Yolanda and Dominick came too. Josephine's son Jason stole the show. He was so cute. A little wiseass he was. Fran's husband constantly teased Jason, and Jason would respond, "Oh, be quiet!" Jason was making everyone laugh.

People were involved in their own conversations. Some of us were looking at Fran's wedding photos, all of us remembering the great time we had. It almost felt like Dad was not sick, as though the cancer had never happened.

Later that night more people came over. Zio Filippo's brother Pino, who is married to my cousin Josephine, my godparents' daughter. Pino came over that night with his daughter Lisa and their son Joey. Josephine and Steven their other son were already living in Florida.

Josephine and Pino's kids were my best friends growing up. We were four of the eight children Zia Maria brought to school each day. Poor Lisa was traumatized when I did not want to go to school one day. My father dropped us off and would not let me go back home with him. I hung on to Lisa on her line instead of mine and cried, "Lisa! Lisa! Lisa!" She was trying to take my gripped hands off her coat but I was so upset and held on so tightly that she was not able to. She was so embarrassed. I still apologize to her for that. Now she gets a kick out of it.

I was so happy my cousins were back in New York, at least for a little while. It made me feel like a kid again. My godmother came over with them. Jason was sticking his tongue out at everyone by then and Zia Maria was scolding him. "You so bad, Jason," she told him. "You a bad boy!" Jason gave her a dirty look and went on with his business. Daddy turned his face and laughed with pride for his grandson.

Dad got nervous then. He felt helpless. All of these people were in his home and he could not entertain them properly. He was nagging Mom. "Is there enough food? Did you buy enough soda? Ask if anyone is hungry if they want anything?!" As if Mom was not already doing that. She was busy running around all day and was ready to fall on her face.

My sister Josephine came into my room where I was catching up with Joey and Lisa. "Susie, Daddy's being nasty. He is working Mommy's nerves like crazy. She is so tired." I felt bad for my mother because I could see her exhaustion. I could not help but laugh, though.

Sarcastically I remarked, "Daddy's home!" Josephine and the others laughed.

"That's for sure!" my sister added.

My brother Benny came over with his daughter Christina, who was just ten months old. Christina was the first niece born into our family. Everyone was fighting over her. Each of us wanted to be the first to hold her. But the poor baby was fussy and only wanted her father. The confusion was upsetting her. Daddy took the baby from Benny's arms and sat her on his lap. Suddenly Christina stopped crying. She stared at Daddy and was fascinated by his eyeglasses. She pulled them off his face and laughed. We all laughed with her. She did that several times and created a rhythm of laughter among all of us.

Then Daddy took off his glasses and kissed Christina's cheeks about a thousand times. *"Che bella sta nipote*! My beautiful girl!" he said.

Benny left the room. Ben's wife was already expecting their next child. I'm guessing Ben realized Daddy might never see the new baby. That is what the rest of us were thinking. But Daddy looked so happy with Christina on his lap as he continued playing the eyeglass game with his grandchild. All the tension suddenly lifted from his face. His grandchildren were the best medicine.

That night and in the days to follow, family and friends filled our apartment. Everyone was anxious to be with Daddy. It was like a race to spend as much time as possible with him, to create as many new memories as time would allow. Zia Carmela came over with her daughter Raffy and *her* daughter Monica. Raffy was like another sister to me growing up, and she was very close to Mom and Dad.

When Fran got married, her daughter was the flower girl in the bridal party. At that time, Raffy was pregnant with her second child. She did not know that it was a little boy, a little boy she calls John.

Zia Carmela sat beside Dad and they talked about their teenage years in Tripoli. They told Raffy stories of her father, Zio Raffaele. What a handsome man he was. In our living room Daddy kept a photo showing him and Zio Raffaele side by side on motorcycles. The two of them looked like models in that black and white. Zio Raffaele and Dad met at work and would often talk or have lunches together. Eventually they became good friends. Mom and Dad were already married and so sometimes Raffaele would come over and visit Battista and his wife. It was there that he met Zia Carmela.

Zia Carmela was a lovely young woman and it did not take long for the young Raffaele to fall in love with her. Unable to resist his charming looks and personality, Carmela soon felt the same affection for Raffaele. They began their courtship and were then married. In Mom's photo albums there were pictures from Zia Carmela's wedding. Zia Carmela looked so beautiful in a traditional long and full white gown. She wore a jeweled crown on her head. They had a three-tier wedding cake with the plastic bride and groom figurines on top.

But shortly after their wedding, Raffaele began having problems with his heart. He was given medication to treat the condition, and it severely damaged his liver. During Zio's illness the newlyweds discovered they were expecting their first child. One month later, Zio Raffaele died. Daddy never forgot his dear friend Raffaele. He liked talking about him. Raffy loved to hear the memories about her father as they came to life in words.

Zia and Daddy told Raffy about the many times they went dancing at the local church when they were younger and still single. Zia Carmela would be out with her brother, Zio Rocco. Daddy would bring his sister, Zia Margherita, while Mommy would be playing ball or reading books with Zio Benedetto, Daddy's younger brother.

Daddy and Zia Carmela also reminisced about the first years they were in America. This was at the end of the sixties, the early seventies, when we all lived in Brooklyn within only blocks of each other. He talked about how we would all squeeze into the four-room railroad apartments for the holidays, and how all the kids got into their pajamas right after dinner. They wondered now how they had come up with the money to fill the table with food and make sure each child got at least one new toy. Dolls for the girls and toy soldiers or boxing gloves for the boys. Some of the men would fall asleep on the couch in the middle of the festivities, exhausted from their days at work. But the women held their own as they cooked and cleaned up, changed the kids and fed them, in between throwing slippers at the rebellious few who answered back or dared to be asked a second time to do something.

Italian mothers can be like Clint Eastwood in some of his western flicks. They never miss a shot with those damn slippers. They must have held secret meetings somewhere after they gave birth to their children. The fathers, on the other hand, only had to *look* at their kids. It was like mental telepathy. *Do what your mother says or I will kick your ass.* All without uttering a word. I was just a baby in the seventies, so I don't know all the stories of what my teenage cousins put their parents through. I just know some stories here and there over time. I usually mix up in my head who did what and when. I just remember thinking when I was a teenager in the '80s and Dad made my favorite pair of tight jeans disappear, *How come Maria and Josephine were allowed to wear those miniskirts or low-rise jeans in the seventies?* Zia Carmela was laughing when I asked Daddy that question once again. I was answered with only *the eyes*. Zia Carmela put her arm around me and kissed my face as I pouted my lips and sat beside her on the couch. Raffy was laughing.

When I was a little older, Zia Carmela and Zio Angelo bought a three-bedroom one-family house. They had a yard and a driveway and two garages. I always lived in an apartment, so their house was a retreat for me. Nonna Giuseppa shared a bedroom there with Raffy. Zio Angelo had the roof taken off one of the garages. Then he put up a pool. Mom and I would take a cab there on summer mornings and spend the day with Zia Carmela and Nonna. I would swim in the pool by myself or with Raffy and her friends. Sometimes I would bring a friend and they would flirt with Rocky or Sal. One Fourth of July, Rocky and Sal brought me with them to a friend's house for the holiday. Since Rocky was older than I, Dad let me go with them. We had a great time.

My doctor's office was a couple of blocks away from Zia Carmela's house. Every time I was ill, Mom and I would go by Zia's house before going home again. Zia Carmela would always give me cookies and soda. She would ask if I wanted some soup or something else to eat. Nonna Giuseppa would put her lips to my forehead to check for a fever. Then she would tell Zia Carmela to give me five dollars from her money. She'd apologize to me for not having more to give. We would watch *General Hospital* in the kitchen. Nonna Giuseppa gave all the characters her own version of their names like *Luca* and *Lola*. She loved to eat bananas and Cheez Doodles. Nonna had no teeth and could smoosh them with her gums.

Zia Carmela always kept a girlish figure. Zio Angelo would come in and tease her as she washed dishes at the sink and he'd whisper in her ear. She would pretend to be annoyed and then shake her head and smile. He never called her *Carmela*. I always remember him calling her *Mughiere,* which means *wife* in Sicilian. He called my mother *Cuniata*, sister-in-law.

That night, we spent hours talking about the past. We laughed and got choked up at times when we thought about Nonna and how much we missed her. Then, even though Dad himself had no appetite, he insisted on feeding everyone else. Before everyone left, he had Mom put together a *spuntino*. That's an Italian snack. No chips and dip, that's for sure. It was usually a big platter or platters of rolled up cold cuts, salami, ham, mortadella. Cheese cut into wedges. Tomato sliced and soaked in olive oil and covered with fresh basil. Then there were olives, green and black, with diced garlic. Anchovies without the bone. There were a few loaves of semolina bread on the table to accompany everything else. Jugs of red wine for the adults and at least two or three kinds of soda for the kids. It was like a little party every night as people came to visit Daddy. That night, as he said goodnight to Zia and Raffy, Daddy patted Raffy's belly and said "Good night for you too, baby!" Raffy had tears in her eyes. Daddy was home. I finally had a good night's sleep.

On another night, Zia Adriana came over with her whole family. It was just like when we were younger. Except now there were more of us. Concetta married John. John was a DJ at a local roller skating rink when I was a kid. They called him *Johnny Sky.* He was so cute, and all the little girls had crushes on him. My cousins and I would brag how he was going to marry our cousin Connie because she was so beautiful, just like him. As it turned out, they did get married and had two sons and a daughter, who are just as gorgeous as the two of them.

John is an only child and his parents, Aggie and Carmine, had become part of the family as much as he had. It was easy to see why John was such a gentleman, knowing his parents. That night Aggie and Carmine came over too. Marina, as usual, was hiding from the video camera or anyone holding a camera. She was such a pretty girl but hated any attention or even compliments.

Little Joey and I were always buddies. We were many years younger than the other kids, so we found ways to have fun when our siblings were out or simply ignoring us. We would hide in the bathroom and find every kind of shampoo or cream and make secret potions. On Memorial Day weekend, we would always pull the same stunt that Stephanie and I had, when we wanted to convince Dad to let me sleep at Zia Adriana's house the night before our picnics. Joey and I would watch television on the living room floor or on the couch while the grown-ups boiled meat and eggs in the kitchen for our traditional Memorial Day feast at Sunken Meadow. As soon as we heard the adults calling it a night, we would pretend to be asleep. Zia Adriana would say the same thing Zia Rosaria would say: "*Stanno dormire. Lascia la bambina per stasera.*"

Dad would look at Mom and she wouldn't answer, "*Va bene.*"

"Okay," Dad would concede. Then once Zia Adriana and Zio Filippo went upstairs to bed, Joey and I would get up and give each other that same high five. We would watch television all night and sneak into the kitchen to raid the fridge.

It's funny how some things never change. Even now, I still call him Little Joey. My Little Joey! At family parties, if Little Joey is around, you will still find me at his side. It's a good thing he and my husband are buddies, too. Joey and I still sit together and eat together. No matter how old we get we act like kids and have so much fun when we're together. We keep each other young, I suppose.

Zia's other daughter is Antoinette. She was the other half of "The Untouchables," along with my sister Francesca back in high school. Antoinette was now engaged to Benny. His full name was *Benedetto*, like my uncle in Italy, not *Bernardo*, like my brother. Just as Stephanie and I had been Zia Rosaria's "Salt and Pepper," Daddy called Antoinette and Fran *Olive Oil*, like Popeye's girlfriend in the cartoon. Like *Olive Oyl*, Fran and Antoinette were both tall and thin.

Concetta, Adriana and Filippo's first daughter, has her godfather's sense of humor. She always has a new joke or funny anecdote to share. This particular night was no different. She held a glass of wine in her hand and said *"Cent'anni!"* the traditional toast, meaning "One hundred years."

Concetta then started her monologue: "Did you ever notice at Italian weddings," she began, "how the video guy passes around the microphone and all the relatives say the same thing? Blah, blah, blah, *cent'anni*! To this guy and that girl, *cent'anni*! Again and again, *cent'anni, cent'anni, cent'anni*!" Everyone including Concetta was laughing, holding their sides laughing. Then she composed herself, stood up, and cleared her throat. As she held up her glass again and said, "All joking aside, for you Zio, *cent'anni* for my *Padrino*!"

Everyone responded with a loud *"Cent'anni!"* and we each took a sip from our glasses.

"Grazie, figlioccia bella! Thank you!" Daddy yelled out. He held out his arms and Connie went to him. He held her face in his hands and kissed both of her cheeks before hugging her tightly. For the first time, Connie was at a loss for words. We all noticed.

Mom and Dad had a special place in their hearts for Connie. The daughter they lost would be the same age as Connie now. Their baby was born in June and Connie was born in August of that year. Only days after my sister was born, the infant fell off the bed. The trauma to her fragile intestines caused her death after only a couple of days. She was in Mom's arms when she died. It was too much for a young mother to take. Mom almost had a nervous breakdown. She was hysterical most of the time and would run around the house searching for the baby. In her mind she would hear the infant crying. At times she would run out and scream on the balcony, convinced that her daughter was alone in the courtyard.

There was no consoling Mom. Then Concetta was born. Zia Adriana would come over with her new baby and mom would snatch Concetta away from her mother. Mom would take Connie into another room and lay down with her in her arms and pretend it was her own little baby girl.

But in the next few months, Mom got stronger. She already had Maria to care for and love, so that helped her to recover. Before she knew it, she was pregnant again and somehow, she knew it would be another girl. She prayed for another baby girl. Daddy painted their room pink in hopes that God would hear his wife's prayers and bring Maria another sister. Then Josephine was born. Through the years, when Mom and Dad looked at Concetta, they could not help but remember their own daughter who would have been the same age as their godchild. She would always be special to both of them.

The same night that Zia Adriana and Zio Filippo's family came over, Francesca had picked up her wedding video. We sat around the living room and watched it together. As the music played Daddy lifted his arms and sang, "Hot, hot, hot!" we all joined him. Then there it was. Connie's evidence. The microphone was being passed around the tables and one of the relatives says, "To the happy couple, *cent'anni!*"

Connie jumped out of her chair and yelled out, "You see I told you, it's true, *è vero!*" Once more we held our sides as our bodies shook with laughter.

* * *

The Holidays

Fran and I decorated the entire apartment. We put up the tree together, as we always had before she was married. There was one time, about two or three years earlier, when I was not at home, that Fran put up the tree by herself. I guess she was trying to be creative. She used lights, icicles, but no garland. She bought a million red apple ornaments and those were the only ornaments she put on the tree. She left all of our family ornaments in the boxes. It looked like an apple tree.

Francesca was trying to be fancy. She had seen a Christmas tree like that in one of the "rich people's" magazines she liked to read. Apparently someone wealthy and famous had a tree like that in their home and Francesca was trying to recreate it. I told Francesca "to get over herself."

I was so furious. Little by little each day I replaced every single apple with one of the traditional ornaments we had collected over the years. By Christmas Eve I had salvaged the Christmas tree and the apple tree was no more. I never let Francesca live that down.

But the year Daddy took sick, this year the tree looked extra special and so did everything else. As I think back now, it probably looked a little cheesy. Besides the tree, we decorated all the walls with those paper cut-outs of Rudolph and Santa and the reindeer. Then we hung garland around the doorways and finished it off with big red bows. We just went a little crazy, but at the time it seemed perfect.

Josephine and I surprised our parents by chipping in for their gift. We could not wait until Christmas to give it to them. We took three of Francesca's wedding pictures and had them mounted on wood. One was of just the two of them, cheek to cheek. The second one was the whole family, parents and children. The third picture was just the children.

My father was beaming when he saw them. He was the one who had the patience for cameras for taking both still photos and video. Growing up, he took tons of photos and filmed family events all the time. In the eighties, when video cameras first came out, Fran went right out and bought him one and as we predicted, Dad started videotaping everything. He taught me how to use the camera too. I learned quickly and actually became rather good at it. As with my swimming performance, Dad would comment, "Oh, my daughter filmed this part. Look how steady her hand is, just like her father's." My response was always to giggle. At nineteen, even though I was mature, when it came to my father I would always be a little girl. Even when I was in the bitchiest of moods, PMS and all, Dad could always make me giggle. I miss that.

* * *

Christmas Cookies

On December 16 of that year, Zia Adriana and Zio Filippo came over to make cookies. Not ordinary Christmas cookies. Sicilian fig cookies called *"cuccidata."* The dough is rolled and filled with figs, raisins, almonds, and a mixture of other ingredients. Zia Adriana was head baker and Mom was her helper. Zio Filippo did the videotaping. Sitting at the kitchen table, Dad supervised, watching as his *commare* combined the ingredients.

As the cookies started coming out of the oven, Dad reminisced about the days his mother baked for the holidays. His eyes were soft with emotion as he spoke of his mother. "When we were kids, there was no money for all of these toys," he said, pointing to the wrapped packages under the tree. "My mother would make *cuccidata* like these in the shape of horses and boats for my brother Benedetto and me. She would make them look like dolls for my sisters. Then sometimes she would make my favorite cookies, *gli torelli*, the plain cookies with the icing on top. I could eat a whole plate of those by myself." Dad always had this faraway look when he spoke of his family.

It was always so expensive to go back and forth to Italy. Dad did go a few times, but had to save up the money first. A couple of times he took out loans to make the trip. There was that one time he took Mom and me and another when he took my brother Benny. When Maria and Joe were getting married, Dad managed to have his parents come to America. When two people from Sicilian families get married, it's always a huge event, and my father insisted his parents be present for the wedding of his first child.

In 1978, Daddy had just started working at the hospital, so money was tight. He had to take out a loan to pay for his share of the wedding. Maria, who was his first baby, was now a young woman about to be married. He wanted her to stay calm and not worry. But she worried anyway, because Maria knew our parents could not afford such extravagance.

Somehow, though, it all came together — the engagement, the bridal shower, and the wedding. It would be the only occasion in which we would all get to spend time together with our grandparents. I did not know it then, but it would be the second and last time I would ever see Nonno Bernardo and Nonna Maria.

Three years later, in 1981, when I was just eleven years old, Nonno Bernardo died. Everyone came over to our house to pay their respects. In all of the confusion, my godmother found me whimpering in the kitchen. When she hugged me I started sobbing. She called out to Daddy, *"Battista, la bambina sta piangere. Gioia mia, the baby is crying!"* Zia stepped aside as I held my arms out to Daddy. His eyes were red and glassy, but he certainly did not cry in front of any of us.

"I am sorry, Daddy," I sobbed, "I am so sorry your father died. I am so angry I never got to enjoy him. Mommy's father died when she was a baby. I only had Nonno Bernardo and he was too far away. Now he's gone, Daddy. My Nonno is gone. It's not fair, *Papà. Non è giusto!"* I whined, bemoaning how unjust it all was.

My father looked away as he pulled me closer. "I'm sorry, Baby. I feel sad too. *Nonno ti voleva bene. Non te lo scordare,"* he said, reassuring me that my grandfather loved me and I should not forget that. How selfish we are as children. Daddy had a broken heart and I was making it worse.

During one of his final visits to Sicily, Daddy had a chance to see everyone. Almost everyone, that is. He spent time with his brother, Zio Benedetto. He spent time with his sisters, Zia Franca, Zia Maria, and Zia Giuseppina. Daddy's sister, Zia Margherita, lived in Northern Italy. The last time Daddy saw his sister Margherita was in the early 1960s when she left Tripoli. She was the only one of his siblings missing from this reunion.

In Palermo, he enjoyed spending time with his mother and loved being with his nieces and nephews as well. When he came home, he had cute stories to tell us about our aunts, uncles, and cousins. He laughed when he told us about his young nephew, Zia Maria's son Gaspare. He was so amused by the boy's sense of humor and mischief. He talked about Zio Benedetto's son, also named for our grandfather Bernardo. His nephew Bernardo made Daddy a beautiful drawing of red roses on a yellow background. It hung in a frame on our foyer wall for years.

Daddy spoke of his older nephews and their families, boasting about how lovely his nieces were. "Sicilian beauties" he called them. He said his sisters and Nonna Maria smiled the whole time he was there. He and Zio Benedetto shared *"barzelette,"* old Sicilian anecdotes, each one funnier than the last. In his nightstand drawer, Daddy kept photographs of that trip. There were photographs of Nonna Maria, Dad's sisters and their husbands and children, and Zio Benedetto and his family. I knew they were in there and would sometimes go and look at them. When Daddy would find me doing this, he would sit beside me and explain each picture. Then he would think back even further, all the way back to his days as a boy in Castellamare, telling me a little bit about his sisters and Zio Benedetto. He would tell old stories of Nonna Maria and Nonno Bernardo. As I sat listening beside my father, I would enjoy every moment of his stories. I especially enjoyed the look on his face when he talked about his family.

Sometimes I felt sad for Daddy because he was so far away from the rest of his family. Even after Zio Benedetto or Zia Pina would call from Italy during our Sunday afternoon dinner, I could see how touched Daddy was to hear the voice of someone from so far away. Then, after getting off the telephone, he would talk about them to all of us. Mommy would always wipe her eyes before allowing the tears to flow. She had been a young girl when she joined Daddy's family. She, too, missed everyone. I know I felt bad that I barely knew my own cousins, and some of them I didn't know at all.

As Daddy shared his memories that night with his friends and wife, the table filled up with platters of *cuccidata*. Then the four friends sat down together to enjoy a holiday toast. Mom filled three glasses with scotch and a fourth glass with milk for Dad, who was still taking medication and advised against drinking liquor.

Dad said, "Filippo, let me try to take some video. I don't know if my eyes will let me but I will try." He took the camera from his friend and got started. As he filmed them he asked, *"Che cosa bevete?"* to have them tell what they were drinking.

They held up their glasses and answered, "Scotch!"

Daddy joked in return. *"Mannaggia, mi fatte dispette!"* pretending to accuse them of drinking to spite him. So with three shots of scotch and one glass of milk, they toasted together. *"Alla salute!"* Daddy said, joyously toasting their health.

On the videotape, the time read 2:43 AM. Just an ordinary night among friends.

* * *

Christina's First Christmas

My brother Benny could not be with us that Christmas Eve. On December 20 we had an early Christmas for Christina. The baby was on the floor by the Christmas tree. She played with the gift wrap instead of the gifts. Everyone bought Christina pink and purple clothes, and she got dolls and baby carriages. We were all so excited to have a little girl in the family. It was nice to watch Benny as he proudly observed our family fussing over his daughter.

But there was a sadness in my brother's eyes that night. How bittersweet this time was for him. As he celebrated his first child's first Christmas, he knew it would be his father's last. Bernardo's relationship with our father was a complicated one. Dad had wanted Ben to be more involved with our family, but as a young husband and father, Ben was struggling with his own family. Not only did he have a wife and a baby, but he had another child on the way. He was also trying to buy his own home and he and his wife were looking out on Long Island. The houses in Queens were too expensive and besides, my brother wanted to leave the city. He was ready, now that he had children to consider. Ben wanted Dad to be proud that he was trying to give his kids a better life in the suburbs. Instead Daddy had been disappointed that his son was looking to move away from the rest of us. In Italian families, the son is second in command to his father. It is a great honor and a great responsibility.

My brother was so spoiled as a kid. Even with the little money our parents had, you had to see what Ben would get for Christmas, just because he was a boy. One year our parents bought him a whole battlefield of soldiers, forts, weapons, and tanks. This elaborate army set included a costume for Ben to wear, complete with a khaki hard hat and a canteen to drink from. Another year he got boxing gloves, a punching bag, and the shorts and sneakers to wear while he was playing.

When I was a kid and was home for the summer I would get so aggravated because Mom would call from work to wake ME up every day. When I answered the phone she gave me orders: "Wake up your brother!" she would say. "Make him coffee and milk and bring it to his room. If he doesn't get up right away make sure he doesn't fall back asleep or he will be late for work." Could you even imagine?

Unlike the girls, Ben was allowed to go out whenever he wanted. He did have a time he had to be home, but it was not ten o'clock. Even when Ben was late, Daddy would always cut him some slack. Well, almost always. There was one time Ben got in BIG trouble, and Francesca and I may never forget that night.

I love telling this story to Benny's kids. He laughs right through the stern look of disapproval he tries to give me as I speak. Bernardo

99

went out with his friends one night. Girls, clubs, teenage boy stuff. He stayed out almost all night, way past his given curfew and even beyond his grace period of being late. By the time he came home, the rest of us were asleep, that is, everyone but Mom and Dad. Mom was in bed praying that nothing bad had happened to her son. She was also dreading the scene that would take place between her husband and son when Ben did get home. Dad was walking back and forth between the living room and Ben's bedroom. He was drinking espresso in the middle of night so he would not fall asleep before his son got home.

Then he looked out the bedroom window and saw Ben staggering down the block and calling "Goodnight!" to some friends who had dropped him off on the corner. Daddy turned off all the lights in the house and sat in the dark on Ben's bed. When Mom asked, "Was that Bernardo?" Daddy answered, "Stay in bed and don't move. I will take care of this!"

But Mom did not listen. She quietly put on her robe and slippers and waited for Ben to walk in. Ben came in the front door and headed straight to his room, grateful that everyone seemed to be asleep. Daddy smelled the alcohol from two bedrooms away. When Ben opened the door to his room Dad stood up from the bed, turned on the light with a pull of the cord and SLAPPED Ben right across the face.

Ben hit the floor. Mom started screaming, "Oh, my God, what did you do?" Daddy walked past her and went to his bedroom.

Fran and I woke up and Fran yelled out, "Oh, my God, Benny is dead! Daddy killed him!"

The truth is Benny was full of it. He pretended to faint. He figured if he stayed down, Daddy would feel bad and save him from another shot. Mom put perfume under his nose to wake him and Benny almost gagged. When Daddy heard Ben coughing and trying to get up he went back into Ben's bedroom. Ben again pretended his legs were weak. So Daddy and Mom helped him onto the bed and let him sleep it off. Daddy went back to his bed shaking his head. Mom was cursing at her son and her husband under her breath. Fran was hysterical and I just turned over and went back to sleep. Do I know my brother or what? I still love that story. It only seemed fair, since Ben never got grounded for breaking curfew, as I did as a teenager. At least I feel better knowing he faced some kind of retribution.

Benny went through a defiant stage when he was about sixteen. What's that phrase? *Boys will be boys!* On the evening before Mother's Day, the phone rang at two or three o'clock in the morning. My mother's heart seemed to stop as she gripped her chest. *"Bernardo, Dio Mio!"* she cried out. She went to grab the phone. Dad was still awake in the living room and grabbed the other line. It was Ben.

"Mamma, it's Mother's Day. Happy Mother's Day. I'm sorry, Mommy. I'm at the police station. I got arrested. I'm sorry, *Mamma."* Dad hung up his line and went into the bedroom to check on Mom. Mom was holding the phone, not knowing for a moment what to do. Daddy got to the bedroom and grabbed the phone from her hand. Benny told him what happened and where he was.

Ben was out with friends at a local club. On the way home they walked past a car dealership. Challenged by a dare, Ben broke the showroom window and went inside. For some reason, a reason he would never explain to his baby sister, he just sat there. When the police arrived, his friends were long gone. No surprise. Mom and Dad had to get to central booking in the middle of the night.

Fran and I had both woken up when we heard Mom crying. *"Mio figlio!"* she was yelling. "My baby." We thought Ben had gotten hurt and so we were crying too. Daddy sent us back to our beds.

"It's okay," he told us. "Your brother is okay. We have to pick him up, that's all. Don't worry, *non vi preoccupare!* Go back to bed."

Fran and I knew that while Mom was worried for Ben, Dad was

both worried and angry. His face was bright red and he was mumbling loudly something in Sicilian, but he was speaking too quickly for us to decipher what he was saying. Then we heard Mom on the telephone. I don't know if she called Maria or Josephine, or both of them. But before I knew it, I heard Josephine talking to Daddy in the living room, only now the adults were speaking quietly and I could not hear what they were saying. Mom would not tell me until I was a grown up what happened that night.

When they got to the courtroom Ben was escorted in with his wrists handcuffed behind him. Dad grabbed a nearby chair so he would not fall. He was devastated at the sight of his boy in handcuffs. Ben was a minor and had no prior arrests. His bail was set at five hundred dollars. Back in the '70s, this amount may as well been a million dollars. Of course, my parents did not have it. Daddy wanted to spare his son's pride and did not want Ben to feel obligated to anyone in the family. He himself did not want to feel obligated nor did he want his son to be judged by anyone. So Daddy went to an outside source for the money. A man from the old neighborhood. He borrowed the money with his own word and made Ben commit to working to pay back every last dollar of it, interest and all.

Ben was released and put on probation. He was never arrested again. It took Ben a while to pay back that money, but he did it. The same day that Ben gave Dad the last of the money Daddy surprised him with a gift. He bought him a really nice watch, a watch that Ben would treasure. I guess without words he was telling Ben, *I understand. I forgive you.*

Daddy loved my brother Ben. He would lecture him all the time about staying away from the wrong people and doing the right thing for himself. He wanted so much for his only son, and my brother would never answer him back. Ben got into some little bits of trouble here and there. He had a few jobs he either lost or quit. It was a wild time to be young.

As some of Ben's friends were getting killed and going to jail, he made a decision. It was time to grow up and get away from the neighborhood grind. The gangs, the drugs, the violence. My brother joined the army. Benny figured that in the army, he could concentrate on getting his GED, see new places and learn new skills. Dad was a little upset at first but understood and respected Ben's reasons. He was proud of his son for wanting to make a future for himself. When Ben sent home the first 8 x 10 photo of himself in uniform, Daddy framed it and hung it on the dining room wall. Daddy would tell his friends at work of the different places in the country and world that Ben would be sent to.

I would bring Ben's letters to school and show my teachers. My brother the soldier. Dad accepted that his son was a man now. He and Mom were both proud and anxious until Ben finished his time in the military and came back home. By the time Ben did get home, I was almost a teenager. I wasn't the chubby little baby he left at home. His first night back he turned to Daddy and said, *"Papà, hai visto a mia sorella.* You saw my sister. I say we lock her in the closet 'til she's thirty!"* The rest of the family laughed as I rolled my adolescent eyes at my brother. He pinched my cheek and kissed it then he hugged me. I was glad my brother was home. Even if I had to give up his room.

But now, Bernardo was a husband and a father and I could see that he was still trying to impress his own father. He was always trying. Ben never graduated high school but earned his diploma while in the service. When he got his driver's license he saved up the money and bought his own car. When he got married, Ben paid for his own wedding. Of course the pressure was on Ben since the day he was born in 1962.

The day Bernardo was born was a holiday for our family and my father's family. He was the first grandson who would carry our grandfather's name. He represented not only a new generation of our family, but also the promise that the family name would continue. After three girls, now there was a male in the family. A son, a grandson.

Nonna Maria worked for a wealthy Jewish family. As she pressed the family's clothes, she shared the news of her new grandson. The wife told Nonna, "What a special occasion! An occasion fit for roses. Roses for his mother." And so Nonna went to see her daughter-in-law and grandson with a dozen long stemmed roses in hand. Quite a luxury for a working family. Mom could not believe it.

Mom's brother, Zio Rocco, saw Nonno Bernardo on his way home from work and congratulated him on his new grandson. "*Zio Bernardo*, auguri! *Finalmente un' altro Bernardo!*" declaring that there was finally *another* Bernardo. Of course, Nonno Bernardo was beside himself. He would not believe he had a grandson, a namesake. He had to see the baby right away himself. When he arrived at Mom's house, he went right to Nonna Giuseppa. Mom was resting after giving birth, without any sedation, to an eleven-pound baby. Eleven pounds.

Nonna was holding the infant. She presented the baby to his grandfather. Nonno Bernardo was overcome with joy. He handed the baby back to Nonna Giuseppa. "Show me," he demanded. "Show me it's really a *boy!*" Nonna Giuseppa smiled as she unfastened Bernardo's diaper. There was the unmistakable proof. Nonno and the rest of the family began to applaud.

Nonno Bernardo went to where Mom was resting and quietly kissed her forehead. Mom looked up at him sleepily and smiled. He took her hand and said, "*Grazie, Silvana, grazie per sta grande gioia!*" Thanking her over and over again for this great joy. Daddy's brother, Zio Benedetto, went directly to see his new nephew after work. He too was so thrilled with the news. He embraced my mother, whom he loved as his own sister, and he too thanked her. "You are the best sister-in-law in the whole world. *Grazie, Silvana, Grazie!*"

Only two months after Bernardo's birth, our grandparents moved back to Sicily. In the 1960s, politics were changing in Africa and foreigners were not as welcome as they once were. As a result, Italian families started leaving Tripoli. But my parents stayed in Tripoli for almost two more years and then decided that instead of returning to Sicily, they would come to America.

* * *

It came time for Ben to get home the night of our early Christmas. It was getting late and Christina was cranky, wanting to sleep. Everyone passed the baby around and covered her with kisses. Ben wished us all a merry Christmas. He came to our father and they embraced. "Merry Christmas, *Buon Natale, Papà*. I love you." Time stood still as we all looked on.

"*Buon Natale,* Bernardo. I love you too." We all turned our faces as we wiped our tears. Dad went into the bathroom and locked the door. Ben fought his emotions as he left quietly with his daughter.

* * *

Christmas Eve

On the real Christmas Eve, my sisters and their husbands came over. My nephews were there too. David, Michael, and Jason were counting the minutes until midnight when they could open their gifts. In the Italian tradition, the table was heaped with all kinds of seafood — fish filet, seafood salad, calamari, baked clams, *baccalà*, the dried codfish that is so popular among Sicilians for the holiday.

Joe G. was making pizza. We all ate and watched television. We teased the kids, saying none of the presents were for them, but they knew better than to believe us.

It was getting closer to midnight and we were all stuffed. We sat around the living room — on the couch, on the dining room chairs, on the floor, in every available space. Even the adults were getting restless. "Let's sing," suggested Francesca. "We could pass the time until midnight."

While some families went to midnight mass on Christmas Eve, our family had a tradition of opening gifts at the stroke of midnight. How I remember being a kid, just as anxious as the boys were that night. Mom would scrimp and save all year so that each of us would have new pajamas and a matching robe to wear on Christmas Eve. Then everyone got one gift to open under the Christmas tree. I was the youngest so I always had one toy under the tree. My brother and sisters were older than me, so they usually got a new sweater or other articles of clothing.

It was great to be the baby, because as the other kids got older and were working, they would buy me gifts as well. So then I got the pajamas, robe, and one toy from Mom and Dad, but I also got other treats from my siblings. Sometimes it was new clothes, new shoes, or sneakers. Other times I got more toys. As a teenager I started getting perfume, music cassettes, books, and makeup. I certainly was not deprived. Perhaps I didn't have the fancy video games that started becoming more popular in the 1980s, but I didn't mind at all. I was quite content with all the wonderful gifts I did receive and most of all I was so happy having everyone together. Christmas was always my favorite holiday.

Mom worked for fourteen years, and usually the factories were open on Christmas Eve. Sometimes she would have to wait for the paycheck she received that very evening to finish shopping for gifts for the family, or even to buy the last of the food. Despite her exhaustion, she came home, changed her clothes, put on an apron and slippers, and started preparing all the fish. Daddy always helped with the cooking.

I guess one of the advantages of having five children is that you do, eventually, get some help with the household chores. Joe G. was great in the kitchen. That year, because Dad couldn't help with the cooking, Joe G, Jack, and Fran's husband were in the kitchen helping Mom with the food. Maria was always cleaning something. Josephine was keeping an eye on the boys and resting her pregnant self on the couch. Fran and I had gone to the mall together that

106

afternoon to buy some last minute gifts. Once all the errands were done, I changed into my new outfit — black leggings and a red and black striped shirt, so that I could take pictures near the tree with the boys. After Dad's surgeries and loss of vision, I became the official new family photographer, although Fran's husband was always walking around with his own video camera. Sometimes we would videotape each other videotaping each other. It was funny. You would hear us laughing the entire time.

We all looked at one another that night when Francesca suggested we sing. "You're such a nerd, Fran," I said to her and everyone was laughing, even Francesca. "Let's just sing," I said. "Let the boys pick the songs."

So that is what we did to pass the time until midnight; Maria, Josephine, Fran, the kids, and I sang. The men just listened and occasionally chuckled or rolled their eyes, but we just kept singing. We sang Jingle Bells, Silent Night, and Rudolph the Red-Nose Reindeer. Then finally Maria yelled out, "Okay, it's midnight!"

The kids jumped headfirst into the presents. We all kissed one another on both cheeks and embraced. We handed out the gifts. The children's gifts first. They were jumping up and down with excitement. We could not help but laugh.

Josephine and Jack disappeared to their apartment without their sons even noticing. They returned about three minutes later and announced, "Wow, look what Santa left next door! New bicycles for the boys!" The room was even brighter than the tree at Rockefeller Center. Those boys were so happy. Daddy's face lit up like a star as he witnessed the joy on his grandsons' faces.

The boys got on their bikes and tried to ride them in the living room. We all laughed out loud and shouted, "No, there's no room in here!" as we each grabbed one of the bikes. We were all kissing the boys and laughing.

We passed the rest of that year in a continuing celebration. We had company in and out visiting Daddy. Some people even came over from the hospital. Daddy was feeling stronger and was in good spirits. He knew that in the new year he would have to face radiation. We all knew and were anxious about it. My Joey was still in Sicily visiting with his grandmother. I was getting restless. He was supposed to come back in January. But then his cousin asked him to be best man at his wedding…in February! It would be another month until I could see him again. I needed him now. There was so much to tell him. I felt so useless and was frustrated and angry. I wanted to save my father. I kept praying. I prayed the radiation would kill the cancer and keep Daddy alive. I prayed and I prayed and I prayed.

Part Three

January, 1990

With the holidays officially over, Daddy's radiation treatments were set up for the middle of January. The dreaded moment had arrived. Dad would get the treatments at the same hospital where he had once worked. His days there as an employee were over and now he was a patient instead. His hair had finally grown back since the brain surgery, but it would not stay on his head very long.

Once the treatments started, Dad's hair came out in clumps. Every time he rested his head on his chair he would leave behind a handful of hair. That was not the worst part of it. We were able to get past that with our jokes and good humor. We teased Dad about the hair loss, trying to make light of it. We called him *Kojak*, the bald cop played by Telly Savalas in the television series.

At that time, I had a best friend named Lisa, whom Daddy treated like one of his own nieces. The two of them were very close, joking all the time. I had the same kind of relationship with Lisa's dad, so in this way, we were more like family than friends. Of all my friends, it was Lisa whom Dad frequently allowed me to visit overnight, and she often spent the night at our house too. She was such a good friend to me the whole time Joey was away in Italy, and now she was really trying to stay close to me during Dad's illness.

Lisa would often come over and have dinner with us and her parents often included me in their family dinners. When Lisa's little sister had her dance recital, I went to see it with the rest of the family. We had a lot of history together and that made it easier for Lisa to be included in our family circle during this especially difficult time.

When we started teasing Dad about looking like Kojak, Lisa joined in and played a joke on him. She came over one day and was carrying a paper bag, which she told Dad was a present for him. When he opened it he found all different flavored lollipops. This was Kojak's trademark. Anyone who watched the show remembers that no matter what Kojak was doing, he always had a lollipop in his mouth.

Daddy handled it with a sense of humor. He grabbed a bunch of those lollipops and laughed out loud, saying "Oh you *really* want me to look like Kojak!" Lisa, Mom, and I were laughing and enjoying the sound of Daddy's laughter. But as he laughed, Daddy started to cough. The side effects of the radiation treatments were wearing him down. The terrible fatigue. He was always so tired. Daddy, who was always so meticulous about his appearance and manners, was constantly spitting mucous into a tissue. Every little laugh or a cough would bring the mucous to his throat. Daddy was so embarrassed and could barely stand people looking at him anymore.

But Lisa just bypassed Dad's cough with a chuckle and said, "I'm glad you like the lollipops. Enjoy." She wanted to give him a hug but Dad was embarrassed that he had just spit up. He hugged her with one arm and turned his face away. Lisa lovingly kissed his cheek and embraced him tightly. She was not offended by the spitting. Like us, she felt bad for him. She cared about him so much. When she let go, she excused herself and went to my room, supposedly to make a phone call.

With the treatments, Dad became very moody. One minute he was putting on a happy face, but it only took a second for him to snap at one of us, especially when we offered him any kind of food. Food repulsed him, and whatever he could get down would leave his body within the hour. He often left the room, walking quickly to the bathroom holding his mouth as he went to vomit. That made him angry, too.

As if the spitting and nausea were not enough for Daddy to deal with, his eyesight had changed too. After the brain surgery, he had tunnel vision and could only see what was directly in front of him. He was often startled when someone spoke from the side of him. He would reach out to pull whoever it was in front of him to see. *"Non ti vedo,"* he would say, admitting that he simply could not see. It was very frustrating for Daddy and heartbreaking for the rest of us.

Daddy was constantly taking deep breaths. How could he breathe well with only one-and-a-half lungs working? The nights were the worst, because Daddy would cough up whatever was left of his lungs. I would sit on my bed holding my knees and listening from the next room. Each time he paused, my heart would stop. I would wait every night for Daddy to fall asleep. Then I would get out of bed. I didn't want my parents to realize what I was doing.

On those nights when Daddy had had radiation treatments, I stopped sleeping again. I would take my pillow and a blanket and camp out on the floor outside his room. I stayed up all night just listening to Daddy breathe. I was so afraid he would die in his sleep. When I would hear Mom get up to use the bathroom, I would quietly and quickly slip back into my room. Mom never noticed me, never knew I was keeping this vigil. I would stay there until the sun came up, somehow believing that the sunlight would protect my father from death. In the early morning, I would catch only a couple of hours of sleep before going to work. I had to live on diet pills and coffee in order to stay awake during the day.

To add to this misery, I desperately missed my Joey. One night I wrote him a letter as I waited for the sun to rise.

Dear Joey,

When are you coming home? I can't take this anymore. I need you

111

here with me. My father is getting worse. He is so sick. You would not even recognize him anymore. I am watching my own father die a little bit each day. I am so mad. I can't stand this. Why Joey, why him? I know you can't answer that. No one can, right?! He is a good man. There are so many bastards in this world. So many sons of bitches. Not my father, Joey. Why is this happening to him? Why now? This man is only fifty six years old. His wife, my mother, is only forty nine years old. Can you imagine her without him?

I need you Joey. You need to come home. Please. I miss you too much. I love you.

Sue

P.S. I am still mad at you for leaving in the first place. I am glad your grandmother is feeling better. Give her a kiss for me. I will kiss YOU myself when you get home. I miss you!

(God bless that old woman — she lived another eleven years.)

Joey called me as soon as he got my letter. "I'm so sorry, Sue. I felt so bad when I read your letter. I will be home soon. I will be there just in time for Valentine's Day." I let out a deep breath.

"Thank God! I can't wait." Now the difficult part was coming. I knew it was time for Daddy to forgive Joey and accept him as part of our family again. Joey was ready and he and I both knew there was no time to waste. We talked about it that day over the phone. I had less than a month to ask Daddy's permission to bring Joey over to the house again. It would not be easy.

* * *

February 7, 1990

The birth of John Eugene. On this day my first godchild was born. Josephine had her fourth son and I, little Aunt Sue, was now godmother. A sonogram technician had made the mistake of telling Josephine the baby looked like it would be a girl, so we were expecting Samantha Josephine. Instead we got John Eugene. After four sons, Jack and Jo decided this one would be named for both grandfathers. John for our father and Eugene for Jack's father.

Jack's father had also become very ill in those last months of the year. His emphysema, which he had for many years, had gotten worse. He was in the hospital when John was born, but Josephine put a photograph beside his bed so he could see what the baby looked like.

Sometimes I think this baby came along just in time, because Poppa Gene was quickly slipping away. When Jack came back from the hospital after John's birth, he walked into our apartment smiling. "Okay, Dad," he said, "you have another grandson. His name is John Eugene for you and for my father."

Daddy's eyes were shining. "Thank you, Jack. Thank you very much. Your father is very proud too, I'm sure."

Jack was just a teenager, when he came into our home and our family. Josephine and Jack met at a factory where they both worked in different departments. The two of them would make excuses to go to the other's department to catch glimpses and flirt. Jack happened to be friends with our cousin Concetta's boyfriend. Jack would come over to Zia Adriana's house with Connie's boyfriend so he could spend time with Josephine. That's how they started seeing each other.

After a while it was understood by everyone that Jack was now Josephine's boyfriend. There was no formal meeting like Daddy had with Joe G. Jack kind of eased his way into the family. Anyway, tradition was not exactly Josephine's way of doing things. That may be why Josephine got her butt kicked the most out of the five of us. By Mom and by Dad, and also by Maria. Basically, Josephine did not want to listen to anybody.

Josephine would also fight with other people to protect her family. Maria was so shy in school, so some of the more popular girls would bother her. Josephine would get angry and beat them up. Some of the big boys would tease the younger boys, but if anyone tried that with Ben, they too had to deal with Josephine. By the time it was Fran's turn in school, everyone knew to stay away from her because they'd have Josephine to reckon with.

Josephine had no fear. Of anybody. She should have feared Daddy, but she didn't. When she got in trouble for cutting school or smoking or boys she would simply run away from home. That was her way of letting Dad know she was not afraid to be on her own if he didn't approve of her actions.

I remember a time when she ran up the block to my cousin Carmen's house. When Carmen called Mom and Dad to let them know Josephine was there, Dad took the phone from Mommy's hand and said four words, "Bring my daughter home." Then he gave the phone back to Mom. Carmen was very close to Daddy and knew he would be angry with her if she did not bring Josephine right home. Carmen also thought Daddy might just listen if she tried to reason with him. So she did as Daddy asked and brought Josephine right back home. Josephine went right to her room without so much as looking at our parents. Carmen sat down with Mom and Dad, speaking softly and trying to reason with them. Of course I was sent to my room and have no idea what that conversation was like.

As crazy as Josephine made Daddy, she was always looking for him. As a little girl she used to call out for *Papà* when she was sick. As a toddler she was furious when Bernardo was born. She hated all the attention Ben was getting just for being a boy. She was a baby herself when she used to steal Ben's bottle right from his mouth. She would take it out of his mouth and throw it over the balcony. Poor Benny would cry because he was a big baby. He was hungry.

I always remind Josephine about the time she almost killed me. I tell her she was probably jealous of me too because I was the baby. But she insists that what happened with me was an accident, reassuring me that she loved me when I was born.

When I was an infant, people still used cloth diapers with safety pins. Josephine was changing my diaper in the bedroom when I took a pin and stuck it in my mouth. As I started to choke on it, Josephine realized what was happening and she started to scream. Daddy ran into the room and saw my face turning blue. He held my little mouth open with one hand and with two fingers of his other hand he pulled out the safety pin. Josephine swears it was an accident, that I had grabbed the pin myself. I still wonder about that one. All joking aside, she reassures me, "No really, Susie, I loved you when you were a baby. You were like a little toy for the rest of us. It was Benny I couldn't stand. So who cares if he was the only boy? Everyone made such a big deal over him!" That's still her defense when we tease her about it.

Josephine got pregnant with David before she and Jack were married. She was so nervous about telling Daddy. She and Jack told Mommy first, hoping she would tell Daddy for them. Mommy was in shock but she refused to tell Dad. They were the ones who got pregnant and they had to tell Daddy themselves.

Daddy was sitting in his chair in the living room. Josephine and Jack sat together on the couch holding hands. Jack opened up and told Dad, "Dad we have to tell you something." he began. Daddy sat up straight. Josephine squeezed Jack's hand. "Josephine is pregnant. We talked about it, Dad. We are going to keep the baby and we want to get married."

Daddy listened without speaking or flinching. Suddenly a big grin crossed his lips. "*Auguri!*" he said as he got up from his chair. "Congratulations, Jack. You ready to be a father? You make me a *nonno?*"

Daddy and Jack laughed and Mom and Josephine were crying through their smiles. "*Grazie, Papà,*" Josephine said as she and Daddy embraced. It was not the reaction everyone was expecting from Daddy.

Later that night Josephine got out of bed and ran to the bathroom. Daddy heard her and went to check on her. The door to the bathroom was open and Daddy saw Josephine vomiting over the toilet bowl. He went over and pulled back her hair, just as he had done when she was a little girl. When she was finished she fell into his arms and started to cry. Daddy's baby was having a baby.

"Wash up and come inside," Daddy said. *"Ti voglio parlare,* I want to talk to you."

While the rest of us slept, Daddy and Josephine spoke privately in the living room. Daddy held Josephine's hand as she still felt nauseous, asking her if she felt any better. She nodded her head. *"Pina, se tu non ti senti pronta non ti devi sposare"* advising her that she did not have to get married if she was not ready. "We could raise the baby here in this house. You and Jack don't have to get married now because you are pregnant. You are both still young. You should be sure this is what you both want. If you really love each other and want to get married, it still doesn't have to be right now if you are not ready."

Josephine squeezed Daddy's hand. She held onto the armrest as she stood up and bent over to kiss him on the cheek. *"Grazie, Papà.* I do love him, Daddy. I want to get married. Jack and I talked about this and we are both sure."

Daddy nodded his head. *"Va bene,"* he began. "If that is what you both want, then your family will help you. We'll be right here to help both of you and to love that baby. *Non ti preoccupare di niente,"* he said, assuring her not to worry about anything.

Four kids later, Josephine still had not left our parents. When she and Jack first got married they had a ceremony at City Hall. Shortly after that, they had a Catholic ceremony at our parish. Mom and Dad hosted a reception for family and some close friends right in our living room/dining room. Jack's twin brother was the best man and our cousin Concetta was Josephine's maid of honor. The two of them had always been close. Jack's brother and Concetta would also be godparents to David when he was born.

Josephine and Jack lived with us for a little while. Mom and Dad gave them Benny's room to sleep in. My very first best friend Melissa lived next door to us with her parents and little sister Nicole. They would be moving soon. Melissa's mom Cecelia told my mother about the move, thinking Mom may want the apartment for Josephine and Jack. Rent Control. That's exactly what happened. When Melissa's family moved away, Josephine and Jack started their married life right next door to us. I was so upset that my best friend was moving away, but I felt better when David was born and I could see my nephew all the time. Melissa and I would visit one another during the summer.

Valentine's Day was approaching. That meant Joey was coming home soon. My love. I could not wait. This was it. Dad and I had to talk. Mom already warned Daddy that I would be approaching him any day now. She told him that Joey would soon be home from Sicily. She also told him that his youngest daughter was very stubborn and very much in love. This was the man she wanted.

Daddy understood that deep down Joey never meant to hurt me. He realized that Joey respected me and loved me very much. He himself was very fond of Joey. He also never doubted our commitment to one another. Daddy knew his youngest daughter was a dreamer. A romantic. He did not want me to give up those dreams.

I had many dreams as a little girl. First I dreamed of being a lawyer. Benny and Dad thought I would be good at that because I always had a defense for every argument. Then I dreamed of being a teacher. In seventh grade, one of my best friends told me I should be a teacher because I was good at being bossy. I always wanted to be an author. Rarely allowed to go out, I was always reading books. Those books took me away to faraway places and on big adventures, all from the comfort of my parents' home.

I was Daddy's baby girl. His American. He wanted me to have the American Dream: the house, the kids, the success. I wanted that too. But there was something else I wanted. LOVE. True, strong love. I was always thinking, acting, and reacting with my heart first, willingly being naïve to the consequences. He knew that about me, my father. He understood my heart. He *was* my heart. My father always told me there was nothing I could not do, and I believed him.

I went into my parents' bedroom one night to speak with Daddy alone. I explained to him what he already knew. Joey was coming home from Sicily. I said, "*Papà*, you know that Joey will be home soon from Sicily. You know I still love him. He loves me too. Daddy, I think you believe that already." Daddy kept fiddling with some wires around his television as I spoke. "*Papà*, please. You know we were seeing each other before he left. I can't wait to see him again. I don't want to lie to you, Daddy. I want him to come here and be part of this family again. I don't want to hide anymore. I love him so much, *Papà*. Please!" I sat on the corner of the bed with my head in my hands.

Daddy sat beside me and put his hands on my shoulders. "*Va bene*. It's okay. Bring Joey here when he comes back. It's OK," he assured me.

"*Grazie, Papà*. I love you, Daddy. *Grazie*." I hugged my father but he said nothing else to me. He answered only with a kiss on my forehead. He stood up and went back to what he was doing. I left his room and went to my own room.

I was lying on my bed with tears rolling down my face. I turned on my side and just started sobbing. I suddenly felt so afraid. Not afraid of my future, but afraid of the day I would lose my father. Afraid that no one would ever dream with me, *for* me, the way my father did. Afraid no one would believe in me the way Daddy did, that no one would ever love me the way he did. And afraid my dreams would die when *he* did.

My dreams had died for a long time after everything my family went through. I could not recall what my goals had been and I had lost sight of my dreams and wishes. I had wanted to be a teacher because I loved to learn and teach, and most of all, I loved children. I knew I wanted to get married and have my own children one day. Then there was my writing.

Occasionally I would write in journals all that I was feeling. Sometimes it was easier to write down your hopes and fears in a private diary than to say them aloud to another human being. I loved to write letters to friends and to my cousins. Basically I loved to write, anything…everything.

I was famous in the family for my poetry. I would write people poems for their birthdays and special occasions. Sometimes my family or friends would ask me to write poems for them to give to other people.

Then three of my poems were published in three different anthologies. I had submitted them after reading a newspaper article. All three poems had been accepted for publication. It was invigorating to see my name and my work in these massive hardcover books filled with the work of a whole community of poets. And to realize that I was one of them. It got me thinking.

This is what I once dreamed of: poetry, teaching, writing. What happened to all of that? LIFE.

It was seven years after high school that I had this magical revelation. So after a year of planning, I got married. My first dream - LOVE. I had found it, now I had to embrace it and cherish it forever. Less than two years into my marriage I was ready to pursue my next dream – TEACHING, or at least getting back on the road toward my true calling.

I had not gone to college, so obviously I did not qualify for my own classroom. I had to compromise. In 1998, I became a special education paraprofessional. I had started a whole new career. I would work alongside a licensed teacher in the classroom as an

assistant teacher. I help set up the classroom every fall. I help
manage behavior issues among the students. There's so much I get
a chance to do. But best of all, I get to work one-on-one with the
children to reinforce the teacher's lessons. I help the students
understand their subjects better. Each time I teach a child a new
word or a new method of solving a math problem, I feel
wonderful. Their enthusiasm for learning warms my heart.

Most little girls idolize pop stars or even fashion models. When I
was a little girl I was most impressed with teachers. *How could they
know so much?* I often wondered. Now as an adult I get to work with
the best teachers ever! Not only to do I have an opportunity to
teach with them, but I can learn from them as well.

In the spring of my first year as a paraprofessional, I went to college
for the first time in my life. The job paid the tuition and I had to
borrow the money to pay for my books. I went to school two days a
week after work. One of the classes I was taking was Writing 101. It
was during that first semester of college that I wrote a narrative
essay about the Father's Day I spent with Mom and Dad in Florida.

My professor was even younger than I was and he was very
impressed with my writing. I got an A on the assignment. And so
unknowingly at the time, I had started writing this very book. But it
would have to wait a little while longer. That was nearly a decade
ago.

My father always told me there was nothing I couldn't do - but he
neglected to mention I couldn't do it all at once.

***

Valentine's Day - 1990

This was the first Valentine's Day that Fran was not there in the
morning, but she had taken care of things ahead of time. Her job
every Valentine's Day was to take the money Daddy would give her
and buy Mom a huge heart filled with chocolates. She would hide
it under our parents' bed the night before Valentine's Day. When

Daddy would wake up, he'd get Fran and me and take us to his and Mom's bedroom. Fran and I would jump on our parents' bed and each kiss Mom while she was waking up.

"Happy Valentine's Day!" we would shout. Mom would smile, her eyes half-open.

"Okay, *aspetta*, wait," she would say. She would go into the bathroom to wash up and return to her room. There on the bed would be the big box in shiny red paper and a big pink bow. Mom would smile. She would read the card. It was from Daddy, but actually signed by Fran. She knew how to sign Daddy's name better than he did. (That came in handy on the days when Fran or I took it upon ourselves to cut school.) Mom would smile and say "*Grazie, Franca*," and then she'd kiss Daddy as his face turned red from laughing.

"*Io lo pagato*," he would say, reminding her that he had paid for the gift. Fran and I would help Mom rip open the package. Instead of our Sunday meatball breakfast, we would have our traditional Valentine's chocolate breakfast, and I would always grab the caramel candies first.

But this year it was just Mom, Dad, and me. Daddy still came into my room to wake me up. I went into the bathroom to wash up and he asked me to make the coffee. Daddy, who had so loved his coffee, was now nauseated by the smell of it. He couldn't go near it anymore. As I made the coffee, Daddy washed up. I heard Mom get up and walk to the bathroom. "What's wrong?" I asked from the kitchen.

"*Niente, niente*," Mom answered, dismissing it as nothing in order not to embarrass Daddy. He was spitting up in the bathroom again.

Daddy brushed his teeth then opened the door for Mom, who later told me that instead of the usual kiss on the lips, this time it was on the cheek. When Mom squeezed Daddy's arm, she pulled back her hand, suddenly startled at how skinny Daddy's arm felt. She had hoped that Daddy hadn't noticed her reaction. Then Daddy went back into the bedroom.

"Susie," he called out to me. I turned off the coffee and went into the bedroom.

"*Mi hai chiamato, Papà? Il caffè è pronto,*" letting him know I heard him, and that the coffee was ready.

"Get the heart," he told me. "Get the heart from under the bed." I did.

When Mom came into the bedroom, Dad was sitting up in bed. I sat at the foot of the bed. Mom went to her side of the bed. She read the card and kissed Daddy's cheek, this time without commenting about Fran signing it.

Daddy and I smiled. "*Ciccia manca quest'anno,*" Daddy said, acknowledging Francesca's absence this year. There was a lump in my throat, so I just smiled and said nothing. Daddy squeezed my hand. Mom tore open the red wrapping paper. Jokingly, I put the bow on my head.

"I could have put this on my head when Fran got married. That headband was so tight."

Mom and Daddy laughed at me. Mom took the first piece of chocolate then offered the box to Dad. With his hand he motioned it in my direction. I took the box and grabbed one of the caramels. Daddy cleared his throat. Mom motioned with her head to take the box of chocolates away.

I stood up from the bed and said, "I'll bring these inside. I'll get you coffee, Mommy." Daddy stood up and walked behind me into the bathroom. When I got into the kitchen I threw that caramel in the garbage and wiped a tear from my face. I heard Daddy gagging in the bathroom. I made Mom a cup of espresso with her usual teaspoon of sugar and brought it to her bed. When Daddy finished in the bathroom, he came to sit with me in the living room. Later

Mom joined us, her empty cup in hand.

"*Grazie,*" she told Dad and me. She kissed us both on the cheek and went into the kitchen.

"Happy Valentine's Day, Daddy," I said.

Daddy forced a smile and answered, "Happy Valentine, my baby." I got up and kissed him on the forehead. I went into the kitchen to hug my mother.

Josephine and the boys came over a little later. Daddy had already gone to lie down in his room and watch television. We took out the chocolate heart and put it on the coffee table to share with the boys. This Valentine's Day I had one more love in my life. My godson John. He was so tiny -- only a week old. I put a tiny morsel of chocolate on his tongue and said, "Happy First Valentine's Day, Godson!" Mom and Josephine laughed. The boys were watching their little brother.

"Look! He likes it!" David called out. We were smiling.

"Well then, I guess he takes after his godmother when it comes to chocolate!" Then I fed him his bottle of formula to wash down the chocolate.

That evening my brother-in-law drove me to the airport to meet Joey, who was returning from Sicily with his whole family. I felt so nervous, with butterflies in my belly. It had been three months since I'd seen Joey's face. That beautiful face. Would he still love me after three months? God, I hoped so. I missed him so much.

I looked up when I heard someone yell, "Susie! Sue!" *There he is. Thank God, there he is.*

"Joey!" I yelled out. He left his luggage in front of his brother.

"Watch this for me!" Then we went to each other, and right in the middle of the airport lobby I jumped into his arms. It was as though no one else were there. My feet were off the ground and Joey kissed me. He kissed my lips, my face, my neck, my face again.

Lips, face, neck, lips. I was laughing with tears on my face.

He put me down gently. As my brother-in-law came closer, he yelled out, "OK! Take it easy! Save some for the honeymoon!" Joey and I looked at him and both laughed. My brother-in-law kissed Joe on both cheeks. Then Joey and I hugged again.

We went over to Joey's family. I hugged and kissed his parents, Tony and Francesca, whom I had called Mom and Dad since I was fifteen years old. Then I hugged and squeezed Joey's brothers too. I loved Joey's brothers, Angelo and Liborio. I knew them since they were little kids. When I would babysit for Josephine's kids, Angelo would call me and we would talk on the phone for hours. He loved to talk about cars and he would tell me about girls in his class. He was particularly fond of this one girl he met in junior high school, named Caterina. "She's beautiful, Sue," he would tell me. Caterina was his best friend Salvatore's cousin. Sal and Angelo had been together so often as kids that Sal had become like another brother to Joey and Liborio. It was because of their close friendship that Angelo was able to keep track of what Caterina was up to as they became young adults.

I went to Joey's house once while Angelo was on the phone with Cathy. "Here," he said to her, "Say hello to my *sister* Susie," and he passed me the phone. She and I chatted for a little while. How sweet it is to think that now the two of them are married. They even have a daughter, Francesca, and a son, Antonio, both named for Angelo's parents.

The first time I met Liborio, Joey brought him along to pick me up at school. Liborio was about eight years old then, and was a miniature version of Joey. A knockout already. The three of us were talking and laughing. We went into the park and sat together on a bench. Liborio stepped over his brother's legs and sat on my lap. He put his arm around me like a big boy then turned to his big brother. "I like this girl, Joe," he said approvingly. "She's pretty. You should stay with her." I kissed the little boy on the cheek and Joey and I laughed.

Then Joey told him, "Hey, be careful! Are you trying to steal my girlfriend? This one's *mine*, Liborio." Liborio kissed my cheek and I hugged him. Then Joey grabbed his little brother and affectionately messed up his hair.

It felt good to finally have the whole family back from Sicily. I had missed Joey so much. So many times in the months that he was gone I wanted to call him or just hold him. So much had happened. He had not seen Dad in over a year. He was going to be shocked when he did see him. I told him what Dad said, that it was okay for him to come over. He smiled at me. We were both a little anxious but felt that things would be all right.

I do not remember the first time Joey came back to our house again, but when he did, he and Dad just acted as if nothing had happened. There was no big discussion or apology, or anything like that. He came in and they embraced, kissed one another on both cheeks and shook hands. As I expected, Joey was startled to see the way Daddy looked now. It was such a drastic change.

"I can't believe it, Sue," he whispered. "He got so skinny." I just nodded my head. Dad had aged so much. Whatever hair was left on his head was white. White peach fuzz.

I hated to be away from Daddy, so the only time I spent out of the house was when I went to work. Joey and I would be at the apartment all the time. Sometimes Dad would not even stay in the same room as the rest of us. He would often go into his room and sleep. It was just a comfort to me knowing I was there in the apartment with him.

My cousin Antoinette and her fiancé Benedetto were getting married soon, and I was going to be a bridesmaid in their wedding party. Now we were getting ready for another family wedding, but it would be somewhat different from the last time we did this. I asked Daddy's permission to bring Joey to the reception. This time I didn't need to beg him; I just asked and he only nodded yes. I kissed his cheek and said, *"Grazie, Papà."* Mom and Dad would not be coming to the reception. There was no way Daddy could sit in a crowded catering hall for four hours with the loud music and the smell of all the different foods. They would participate by going to the bride's parents' house the morning of the wedding and there they'd see Antoinette in her wedding gown.

* * *

Antoinette's Wedding – March, 1990

On the wedding day, which took place the first weekend of March, it was freezing outside. I got dressed at home and had to put a heavy coat over my turquoise dress that lay off my shoulders. It was actually one of the nicest bridesmaids' outfits I had ever worn. It was a two-piece suit. A long fitted skirt and a beautiful jacket with a sequined pin on the waist. We each wore a sequined comb as a hairpiece.

Antoinette and Ben had put together a very attractive bridal party. Ben had his brother and sisters and Antoinette had her brother and sisters. The rest were cousins and friends. Of course, as with every previous family wedding, Antoinette's younger brother Joey and I were partners. We loved that. At least we knew who we would have to dance with and take pictures with all day.

Dad insisted on putting on his suit to see Antoinette at her home before the wedding. It was so big on him. I think it was the same suit he had worn at Stephanie's wedding less than a year before. When he wore it then the jacket lay nicely on his broad shoulders. Mom tightened his belt around the waist and now had to put a heavy sweater over his dress shirt so the jacket would not look so big. He wore a cap on his head so that he would not be the bald man in the wedding pictures. Everything about Dad had gotten smaller, and even his glasses seemed to take up half of his face.

When Mom and Dad got to the bride's house, all of us bridesmaids were with Antoinette in Zia Adriana's bedroom. We were running off a checklist as Bette Midler's "Wind Beneath My Wings" played in the background. *Something old, something new, something borrowed, something blue.* The bride was good to go. Antoinette was stunning, with her big, bright blue eyes, perfect hair, and great figure. She was just beautiful that day, and still is today, four kids later.

Yola and Dominick's daughter Alex was Antoinette's flower girl. She was just as lovely as the bride herself. Alex was thinking it was her wedding day as well. After all, she and Connie's son Jeremy were walking down the aisle together at church. She would have the same bouquet as Antoinette, only smaller, and wore a miniature version of Antoinette's wedding gown. That little girl was convinced! Jeremy also looked like an adorable little groom in his tiny tuxedo. They made a splendid pair.

I don't know who it was, but someone managed to videotape Mom coming into the bedroom and the bridesmaids heading downstairs to prepare for the photographer. Mom had tears in her eyes when she saw Antoinette in her wedding gown. *"O, che sei bella, Gioia mia. Sei bellisima!"* exclaiming how beautiful Antoinette looked.

Antoinette hugged Mommy. *"Non piangere, Zia,"* she said, imploring my mother not to cry. "Please. Don't get me started."

Everyone had told Daddy to wait downstairs for Antoinette, but, he walked up the stairs to Zia Adriana's bedroom, holding onto the banister and taking one step at a time. Zia Adriana walked up behind him. Together they went into the bedroom, where Mom was fussing over Antoinette's veil and fixing the back of her gown. When Daddy walked in, Mom stopped and looked up. Antoinette looked up too.

"Zio Battista!" she cried out. Then she started to weep. She went to him and they embraced. Daddy rubbed Antoinette's back gently, while Mom and Zia Adriana wiped their eyes. Antoinette did not want to let go of Daddy and he did not let go of her.

"Non piangere, Antonietta," he said softly, telling her not to cry. *"Ti stai sposare. Nianche vuoi semprare brutta quando Benny ti vede in*

chiesa." They laughed. Daddy was teasing Antoinette, advising her to stop crying so as not to look ugly when Benny would finally see her in church.

Zia Adriana and Mom took some pictures of Daddy and Antoinette. Then the four of them made their way down the stairs. Antoinette came down last to make her grand entrance into the dining room. As Zio Filippo watched his daughter walk gracefully down the stairs, his eyes sparkled. He extended his hand to Antoinette as she reached the bottom step. "You look beautiful, Antonietta, beautiful!" Zio and Antoinette hugged each other.

"Thank you, Daddy. You look so handsome." Everyone was watching them. The photographer had arrived by then and was ready for the bride and her parents in the living room, near Zia Adriana's lovely fireplace. We have a million photographs in front of that fireplace -- Zia's family, our family, little Joey and I dressed up for Halloween. Now it would serve as the background for Zia and Zio to take photographs with their youngest daughter on her wedding day.

First the photographer said, "Okay, let's get one with the bride and her proud Daddy!" So Antoinette and Zio Filippo were cheek to cheek. I looked at them and tears welled up in my eyes. My throat felt like it was closing. I turned and walked quickly up the stairs with my head down to avoid anyone's eyes. I made it to the bathroom but there was no time to lock the door behind me. I put my head down on the counter in front of the mirror and started to cry.

Suddenly Marina, Antoinette's sister, was behind me. She turned me around and hugged me. She squeezed me tight and said "Oh, Susie, I know, Baby, I know." We both cried. It took us another fifteen minutes to fix our makeup. We went down separately so no one would question where we had been.

The photographer was from the wedding center where I worked. While the others got prepped for pictures he called me into the living room. "Come on, Sue," he said. "Let me take some shots of you alone. No charge to your cousin! Don't worry." I smiled.

He handed me a bouquet from the box and had me pose in front of the bay window of Zia's living room. Then in front of the mirror in the entrance way. And of course in front of the fireplace. Mom and Dad were watching. Daddy put his hand on Mom's elbow. Mom told me Daddy had whispered in her ear, "*Guarda mia figlia. Guarda che bella la nostra baby,*" delighting in how pretty their baby was. I smiled when Mom told me. I went over to Daddy, who was sitting now in a chair. I kissed his cheek as he patted my arm and smiled at me.

Mom and Dad went straight home. Joey would come to see me walk down the aisle at the church and would then meet me at the reception with my brother Ben and his wife. Maria and Joe would be at church and the reception and so were Fran and her husband. Josephine was home with the boys and with Mom and Dad. I wasn't as nervous as I had been at Francesca's wedding but I did get choked up when the organist played "Ave Maria." That was always Mom's favorite part of weddings; it always makes her cry. I couldn't help but miss her and Daddy.

When we took pictures outside of the church, as everyone threw birdseed at the bride and groom, we were trembling. Our jackets were left in the car. The party began in the limo as we sipped champagne on our way to the local hot spot Antoinette and her new husband had chosen for their reception. The catering hall had a reputation for being extravagant and it certainly lived up to the hype for this occasion.

The reception was amazing. There were all different kinds of foods and an open bar. The band played a variety of music. My friend the photographer took some pictures of Joey and me at the reception. The two of us had a great time dancing together with my cousins. Ben's wife was dancing with a rum-free piña colada in her hand, shaking her pregnant belly on the dance floor. My sister Maria and

I were laughing with her. Many of the cousins had come up from Florida for the wedding. It was so much fun. Everyone asked about Mom and Dad, and sent their best wishes of course.

Finally, the highlight for me at Italian weddings. When the bride dances with her father. A moment that I knew I would never have. I had thought I was prepared to get through this day. I had Joey's arms tightly around me, holding me together and I secured a spot in the front of the crowd so I would not miss any part of it. Zia Adriana and Maria were beside me. Antoinette chose the same song Fran had for her wedding when she danced with Daddy — "O, My *Papà.*" Everyone was in a circle around Zio Filippo and Antoinette on the dance floor as they had their special moment together.

As I watched Zio and Antoinette, I was reminded of Fred and Ginger doing those delicate and graceful dances I had seen when Daddy and I watched those old movies. Mist rose up from the dance floor, creating a dramatic and romantic effect. Zio twirled his daughter all around the floor, and Antoinette kissed her father's face every time they were cheek to cheek. Tears were coming down her cheeks right through the big smile on her lips. Zio was smiling and handling his daughter like a princess, his own little princess. At the end of the song Zio twirled Antoinette around and around and around while their arms were wrapped around one another. It was spectacular. Then Antoinette kissed her father a million times on his cheek while Zio just beamed. It was just how Francesca and Daddy had done it only a few months earlier.

Everyone was cheering for them at the end of the song. Maria and I were crying and laughing at the same time. Zia Adriana had her arms around Maria's shoulders as she too smiled right through her own tears. We all had a wonderful time, but how could we not feel the absence of Mom and Dad?

***

Farewell to Poppa Gene

Poppa Gene, Jack's father, took a turn for the worst in early March.

Because he could no longer breathe on his own anymore, the doctors put him on a respirator. His wife and their kids were at the hospital night and day, never leaving his side. On March 17, Jack's father passed away from complications brought on by his emphysema.

Daddy was sitting in his chair when Jack came in from next door, his eyes red from crying. As he walked into the living room, Daddy stood up. "Jack, what is it?" he asked. "What happened?"

Jack shook his head. "He's gone, Dad. My father's gone."

Daddy and Jack walked toward one another and embraced like two friends, two brothers. "I'm sorry Jack," Daddy said. "Your father was a great man. A great man."

How poetic it was that a proud Irish man should pass away on St. Patrick's Day. I went to Aunt Joanie's house as soon as I heard the news. I found her sitting in a chair in the kitchen. As she looked up at me, I went to her and dropped to my knees. I lay my head on her lap and began to cry. She too was crying as she smoothed back my hair and gently rubbed my back. "He thought of me…" I said softly and appreciatively, "… at Thanksgiving… he thought of me. He would not let me be alone. He was so nice to me, so great. I'm so sorry. I am so sorry."

The loss of Poppa Gene was terrible for Jack's family. Josephine was devastated. She loved her father-in-law so much. He called her *Phina*, short for Josephina. He always looked out for her and the kids. If Jack went out for a few drinks and wasn't home by the time it got late, Poppa Gene knew where to find him. He would call the club that Jack frequented and have someone get him on the phone. Never mind that Jack was a grown man—his father would order him, "Jackie, get the hell out of there! Get home to your wife and your kids!" Jack had a smile and misty eyes as he spoke of his father, remembering all the times he forgot Jack was an adult. Jack did admit he would listen to his father, at least most of the time.

For the boys, the death of their grandfather was a huge loss. Poppa

Gene adored his grandchildren. They were his pride and joy. The boys loved him so much, too, and always looked forward to their visits at Poppa's house.

Poppa Gene's funeral was fit for a president. As a Korean War veteran, he was entitled to a military burial. His wife made sure he got one. She wanted "Taps" to be played at the cemetery, but insisted it be done by a soldier in uniform with a real trumpet, not played on a tape recorder. There was also a live gunfire salute and then the folding of an American flag that covered the coffin. The flag, folded into a neat triangle, was then respectfully handed to the widow from the white-gloved hands of a military officer. It was an awe-filled event, like something from a movie.

Poppa Gene was the father of six children — five boys, and one girl. In addition to his family, there were many big strong guys from the old neighborhood there, people who knew and respected Gene. Once the soldier began playing "Taps" and the guns started shooting, there was not a dry eye at that cemetery. Another day in my life that I will never forget.

***

Joey's Birthday

The third week of March brought Joey's twenty-first birthday. It was hard to believe we had already been together for four years. Of course we'd had intervals of being apart, but it had been four years since I fell in love with him, and five years since our first kiss, which stole my heart.

Shortly after Poppa Gene's funeral, Daddy got really sick. He was in the hospital now with pneumonia. Mom was spending her nights there, again unwilling to leave Dad alone. She was sleeping on chairs at Daddy's bedside, and I was at home, barely sleeping at all. Many nights, Josephine slept at our apartment with the kids, just to keep me company. Baby John was still waking up every few hours for a bottle. That tiny little boy was so eager to grow. I wanted Josephine to get some sleep, so I would get a bottle ready and bring

Johnnie into the living room to feed him. I would give him his bottle and rock him on Daddy's chair. I would hold him in my arms and just look at him. He would look up at me and I would tickle his chin. I love the sounds babies make when they first start smiling at you and kind of gurgle and giggle. I would give him tiny little kisses on his soft little cheek. He would look at me tenderly, as if he knew I was sad. How could an infant understand that? Maybe babies know more than we think. I would hold him and he would fall asleep, and even hours later I didn't want to put him down. Perhaps he was just what I needed at this trying time of my life.

The day after Joey's twenty-first birthday would be Jason's fourth birthday. We planned on having a cake for the both of them soon. On Joey's actual birthday I had to work. Joey picked me up from work and we went back to the apartment so I could give him his gift — a white Sergio Tecchini athletic suit with blue and red striping. Everyone was wearing them that year, and I knew Joey had wanted this particular style because I saw him admire it in a store once.

Joey's mom was having a cake for him that night and he really wanted me to be there. I wanted to be there, too, but first we had to go see Daddy at the hospital. Once again, he was a patient at the hospital where he had worked.

When we got there, Daddy was sitting up in his bed. Despite his pneumonia, he was still trying to be strong, especially when people were around. He wished Joey a happy birthday and asked what our plans were for the evening. "You didn't have to visit me on the day of Joey's birthday," he told me. "You could have come tomorrow."

"No, Daddy," I said emphatically. "Joey wanted to see you for his birthday. He wanted to show you his present."

Joey stepped in front of Daddy. He had changed into the Tecchini suit at the apartment so he could show everyone what I got him.

"Look Dad," he said proudly, "Look what Susie bought me for my birthday. *Ti piace*, you like it?"

Daddy nodded. He touched the sleeve of the jacket. "*È bello, Joe, ti sta bene. Auguri*," he said approvingly.

As Daddy and Joey were talking, I heard a familiar voice in the hallway. It was Daddy's good friend Giuseppe. He came into the room and gave his usual friendly hello. Opening his arms, he said, "*Susanna, bella mia!*" and hugged me. I gave him a tight hug and a kiss on the cheek. Daddy called out to me. "*Susie, vai in casa di Joe che sua madre v'aspetta. Sta venire la mamma ora e gia c'è lo la compania.*" Daddy was reminding me that Joey's mother was waiting for us for his birthday celebration to begin. He reassured me that Mom was on her way and he had company now so it was okay for us to go.

Joey said goodbye to Daddy and Giuseppe, and then went out in the hallway to wait for me. Daddy motioned to his friend to wait in the hallway for a moment. So Giuseppe went out to speak with Joey. Daddy held my hand when I kissed him on the cheek to say goodbye.

"Susie, tell Mommy to get a card for Joe. Tell her to put some money in it for his birthday and give it to him when you have the cake for him and Jason." I looked at him and smiled. Then I kissed him on the cheek again.

"It's okay, *Papà*. Mommy already gave Joey his card at the house. We went there before we came here. *Grazie, Papà. Grazie.*" I hugged my father and left the hospital with Joey.

Giuseppe and Daddy had been friends a long time, before I was even born. Their friendship started back in Brooklyn, when they were neighbors in the same apartment building. They wore their hair the same way, although Giuseppe's hair was lighter than Dad's, and as far back as I could remember, they even wore the same cologne.

Giuseppe is an attractive man who is always well dressed and has a classy air about him. He is also a warm and loving person, and he loved us as though we were family. He has known me almost from the moment I was born, when he first saw me as a baby in that Brooklyn hospital where Daddy worked all those years. Giuseppe had been at Daddy's side that day, waiting for my arrival.

Giuseppe was so present in our lives that as a toddler I would sometimes confuse him with my father. When we went to Italy, Giuseppe was there too, visiting his own family. When we arrived in his town, I saw him and yelled out, *"Papà! Papà!"* Once, when Daddy was in Italy by himself, Giuseppe and his wife came over to check on us. Since Daddy was not there, again I mistook him for my father and squealed, *"Papà! Papà"*! It seems that no one ever told me what to call Giuseppe, and since I always saw him with Daddy, it was easy to label both men the same way. After all, they had the same haircut, they smelled the same, and they both loved me. I guess my little heart told me to call Giuseppe *Papà*.

My husband was amused recently when Giuseppe told him these little pieces of our past. The two of them brought their cars to the same mechanic on the same day. Giuseppe still drives the bright red car he drove the year I was born. I think that's the year he bought it. It still looks brand new. He is still so handsome and so loving. They got to talking while they waited for their cars, and that was when Giuseppe shared these sweet memories with him.

Every year there is an Italian feast on Fresh Pond Road that lasts about three days. I go there at least once every year in hopes of seeing Giuseppe, and I usually do. As I walk through the crowded and colorful streets, I look in all directions for Giuseppe. Then I hear that voice from my childhood calling out, *"Susanna, bella mia!"* The tears come to my eyes as soon as we embrace. Giuseppe notices and squeezes my cheek.

I always think of Giuseppe and Daddy sitting in our living room. I was barely seven years old when I would make Daddy and his friend espresso. Daddy taught me how to use the coffeepot. How much water on the bottom, and how much coffee. He taught me how to sweeten the coffee when it was done: one and a half tablespoons of sugar for every pot of espresso. I would pour the coffee into the demitasse cups, placing a tiny spoon on the matching saucer. Even though the coffee was already sweetened, as a courtesy I would still put the sugar bowl on the table in case anyone wanted more. "*Grazie, Susanna bella!*" Giuseppe would say to me and then he would squeeze my cheek. Daddy would look to the side and smile.

If Mom would get up to make the coffee, Daddy would stop her. "*No, voglio che mia figlia fa il caffè. Viene troppo buona quando lo prepara mia figlia,*" he'd say, telling Mom he wanted me to prepare it because he knew it would be extra good. My face would turn red because I knew he was teasing me and showing off his little daughter, who could already make good coffee.

Daddy also taught me how to disinfect the entire apartment. He knew how to bribe me when I was a teenager. The deal was, if I helped my mother clean the house on Saturday morning and afternoon, I could go out on Saturday night. But by the time we finished cleaning I had no energy to go out. "I'm going out *next* Saturday night!" I would yell out from the bathtub.

"Oh, *Gioia*!" Mom would sympathize. "She's too tired to go out. You tricked her."

Daddy would laugh and Mommy would motion for him to be quiet so I wouldn't hear him. I always did. "I'm sorry, Sweetheart, but you did a great job! *Ti puoi sposare ora,*" he'd say, advising me that I could get married now. "You know how to clean the house!"

I would hear him laugh again. "Yeah, thank you Daddy!" I would yell. "Who will I marry when I am never allowed to go out with a boy? Besides when I get married, I am going to pay someone else to clean my house!"

Daddy and Mom would laugh out loud. Daddy would make a circular motion with his hands. "Okay, *vediamo*, we'll see!" he would call out to me, the two of them still laughing. I would be smiling as I lay back in the tub. I was thinking of that just the other day, as I scrubbed the toilet bowl in my "marital" bathroom.

* * *

Joey and I had mixed feelings the night of his birthday. We were so happy to be together. Now with Daddy's blessing we did not have to hide our relationship anymore. As we ate cake and celebrated with Joey's family, our thoughts were with Daddy. We told Joey's mother what Daddy had said about giving Joey a birthday gift from him and Mom. She looked at Joey and me and shook her head. As she put down a tray of cups she made the sign of the cross with folded fingers and sent a kiss up to Heaven, just like the Italian ladies at church do when they send their prayers up to God.

* * *

First Born

Daddy was home again by the end of March, but he was rapidly getting sicker and more frail. He never left the house anymore. There was more than one person to worry about, to pray for. My sister Maria was having surgery in the city that month. After ten years of battling endometriosis and trying to have children, there was nothing more to do. Several previous surgeries had caused too much damage to Maria's uterus and ovaries. The doctors advised that Maria, only thirty-two years old, have a hysterectomy to avoid any more danger to her health.

This was such sad news because if any woman in the world should have had children, it was Maria. She was a natural mother since the time she was just a toddler. While other little girls played "House" and "Mommy" with their dolls, Maria was already cleaning a real house and taking care of her siblings. At fourteen years of age, Maria dropped out of school. She wanted to stay home and watch me because Mom, who could not afford to stay home anymore, wanted to go back to work. Anyway, Maria hated school and wanted to be with her baby sister. So while Mom was at work, Maria would feed me, change my diaper, and dress me up in pretty clothes. I was her little doll. While I took a nap, Maria would dust the apartment and wash clothes. Mom would come home and find me all clean and dressed up and the table set for dinner. Whoever got home first cooked dinner – sometimes it was Mom and sometimes Dad. But it was Maria who had done all the background preparation.

When I was old enough to start school, Maria went out to work. At twenty-one, she got married to Joe G. I remember the day she arrived back from her honeymoon in Florida. Even in that first month of her marriage, Maria prayed she was already pregnant. She and Joe G. both loved kids and knew they wanted a family. But as the months went by and Maria was not getting pregnant, the doctor visits began. After some time and several consultations, Maria was diagnosed with endometriosis, a thickening of the uterine tissue. Desperately wanting children, she began treatment. There was no guarantee that she would be able to conceive but she took the risk and had several surgeries. It was painful, both physically and emotionally, especially for two people who worked hard and would have made great parents. Ten years later, Maria's condition had only worsened and she was advised to have the final surgery, a hysterectomy.

All those years I never knew what was going on. I was only a child, and Maria did not discuss her condition or her painful experiences with me. Even at the age of nineteen, I could not possibly comprehend the tragedy my sister endured. It was not until I was thirty and had my first miscarriage that I had an inkling of what she had gone through.

When I learned that I was expecting, I was thrilled. My husband and I had been married almost four years by then but had only been trying to conceive for a couple of months. Every month of waiting felt like a year. Finally, there was a positive pregnancy test. I took three to make sure. Then I went to the doctor for a blood test, which confirmed it.

I asked my big sister to be godmother to my first child. She was so proud and so happy. "My baby sister is having a baby!" I heard her tell her friends. She began immediately making plans for her future godchild. But in the eleventh week of my pregnancy I went for a routine sonogram and there was no heartbeat. The baby was gone.

I had had all the symptoms of a regular pregnancy, went through the first trimester fatigue, the nausea, vomiting, the headaches. Even my belly had begun to swell in the last couple of weeks. But my body was deceiving me because there was no more baby.

The day after the sonogram and the terrible news, Maria visited me. She came to my house before I had the procedure that would take away what ever was left of my unborn child. I was actually glad the doctor did not do the procedure right away, just to still have the beginnings of my baby inside me for a little longer. Maria sat beside me and held my hand but I could not even look at my sister in the eye. For the first time in my life, I understood what she must have felt all those years she was trying to conceive — pain in her body and a void in her heart.

She held my hand and kissed me on the forehead. "I'm sorry, Baby. If anyone understands what you feel right now, it's your big sister. I know you're hurting and you are angry, too." Then she hugged me. As we held on to each other, she cried, "It's not enough what *I* had to go through, but now *this* for my baby sister!" We held on for another minute. When we let go she looked at me and squeezed my hand again. "You can't give up," she told me. "You can't give up. You are still young. The doctor said you could try again in three months. You try again in three months! You are going to have a baby! I will wait a little longer for my godchild. Then when he's born we will love him even more."

I smiled through my tears and said, "I won't give up, Maria. We will have our baby."

Thankfully, a year later, God gave me a healthy baby boy. I gave Maria the godson she was waiting for. She loves him as much as she promised me she would. I did not think it could be possible for me to love my sister any more than I already did. That experience brought me closer to her heart, closer in understanding what she must have been going through all those years. I never respected her strength more than in that time of my own life.

And so with Maria having surgery, my father insisted on going to the hospital to visit her. Mom helped him bundle up and the three of us went together. When we arrived, Joe and Dad embraced without saying a word to each other. Mom hugged Joe and the tears welled up in her eyes. I fought my own tears as I hugged and kissed my first brother-in-law on the cheek. He went to the other side of Maria's bed to give Mom and Dad room to be near Maria. I saw my sister wincing in pain as she tried to sit up. She looked at Daddy and pouted like a little girl. She extended her arms out to Daddy and cried out, "*Papà, Papà.*" Daddy hugged his daughter and they cried together. It was the only time in my life I saw tears on my father's face.

I stepped outside of the room and lay my head against the wall, trying to compose myself. I did not want Maria to see me crying, but she noticed. She looked at Mom and said, "*Ma, vai vedere per Susie, forse sta piangere,*" telling Mom to check on me.

I heard what she said and walked back into the room. "Are you Okay, Sue?" she asked me. I nodded my head. I gave her a kiss on the cheek and wiped her face still wet with tears.

"Am I OK? Are *you* OK?" She nodded her head but could not give me an answer. I squeezed her hand.

Mom had Daddy sit in a chair near the bed. She gave him a glass of water. Mom could not conceal her grief for Maria. The tears on her face were hard to hide, even though she kept wiping her face and taking deep breaths.

Daddy held Maria's hand the whole time. Occasionally he would caress it and even pretend to slap it affectionately. He would force a smile in order to make Maria laugh. She would smile at him, but then her eyes would get glassy again. Then Daddy would squeeze her hand and Maria would force a smile and wipe her eyes. It was a tender little exchange that did not need any words.

When it was time to leave, Joe came around the bed and helped Daddy stand up. Daddy stood over his daughter, once more embracing her and holding her face, he looked her in the eye.

"Coraggio figia mia, coraggio!' he said. He choked on his own words and started to cough, shaking his head and waving us off with his hand as we began to fuss over him. He hugged Maria one more time. Then we left her to get some rest.

As we walked down the long white corridor of the hospital, Daddy's shoulders shook as he fought back his grief. His firstborn baby was suffering. This was a pain that no kind of medicine could heal. His first son-in-law, who had become a son to him, was suffering too. Not only could Daddy not make things better for them but he was too ill to comfort them the way he wanted to.

He did not say a word at all on our way back to Queens. When we got home he went right to his bed. Mom walked around the apartment crying the whole night. *"Mia figlia. Mia figlia,"* was all she could say. *"Mia baby no avrà mai il suo baby. Il suo sognio. Mia figlia,"* she cried, grieving for her daughter who would never have her dream come true, who would never have her baby.

The heavy dose of medication and the after effects of the anesthesia helped Maria sleep through that night. When she awoke the next morning she was still very groggy. "How are you, Honey?" a nurse asked. Maria bit her lip as she tried to sit up in her bed. "Take it easy, Honey," the nurse advised. Maria reached for her tray, in need of a cup of coffee. She was hoping the whole surgery had been only a nightmare, that it had not really happened, that the doctors had not ripped out her last hopes of having her own child.

"Did you sleep well?" the nurse asked, interrupting Maria's thoughts. It was real. "You were crying," the nurse told her. "You were crying in your sleep and you kept calling out for someone. Do you remember, Honey?" She spoke as she checked Maria's vital signs and the I.V. in her arm. Maria shook her head. She could not remember anything, thanks to the medication. "I'm not sure if I heard you right," said the nurse. "It sounded like you were calling out, *Papà! Papà!* Is that what you call your father, in Italian, I mean?"

Maria nodded. She sank down in her bed and pulled the covers up to her neck. She had been calling out for Daddy in her sleep. Now she remembered his visit yesterday after her surgery.

Maria has never loved anyone in her life the way she loved our father. He was the greatest strength she had. While Maria was fighting desperately to have children, Daddy never let her feel sorry for herself. When one doctor gave her bad news, he made her call someone else. When Maria would get depressed or frustrated he would say, "*Coraggio!*" just as he did that day in the hospital. "*Corragio!*" Where would she find her courage when he was gone? How could she get through anything without the strength Daddy gave her, without the friendship she had with him?

Daddy used to call Maria every day from work. "Hello, Sweetheart," he would say when she picked up the telephone.

"Hey, *Papà*," she would answer. Then he would tell her about his day at work and ask how she was doing. Maria would ask him about the specialty dishes she wanted to cook for Joe.

As Maria went through ten years of doctors, she took countless train rides with Daddy into Manhattan to see specialists. Daddy was the only one who could get through to Maria. When Maria has her mind set a certain way, there's no changing it, but Daddy had his own way of reasoning with her. He treated Maria differently from the rest of us. He joked with her, but in a more delicate manner because she was more sensitive than the rest of us. Daddy understood that. Daddy demanded the rest of us kids treat Maria with the utmost respect.

She smiled to herself as she thought of Daddy and fought back tears. Immediately following her release from the hospital she went to see him, defying everyone's instructions to go home and rest for at least a few days. She felt she had to be strong for her father now. He needed her, and she had to be there for him.

Even Joe G. reacted the same way. He was often at the apartment after work and spent as much time as he could with Daddy on the weekends, putting his own grief aside to be a strong shoulder on which his father-in-law could lean.

Part Four

April, 1990

Spring had officially arrived. The birds were chirping and the trees were green again. Everyone was excited because the World Cup would be played in Italy that summer. Everywhere you went there were posters and banners that read *Italia '90*. There was even a song about it that was featured on that year's Sanremo Festival in Italy.

One day I had committed to coming home from work early to watch my new godson, who was bigger and cuter with each passing day. As a family, we operated like a team. Mom was out that day, so Josephine stayed with Daddy. But when she had to go out to pick up the kids from school, I would jump in. It was a good plan, except that I got so busy at work that I lost track of time.

Josephine had to go, so she left the baby with Daddy. When I got home, I found baby John and Daddy on Daddy's bed. My father had a big smile on his face as he just stared in wonder at his namesake. "Your godmother's here," he told the baby.

I kicked off my shoes and sat beside John on the bed. "Hello, *Figlioccio!*" I said to him. I lay beside him on the bed and kissed his tiny cheek. "How is my beautiful godson today?" He looked up at the sound of my voice and gave me a smile. Daddy and I laughed.

"I'm sorry, *Papà*. We got so busy today," I apologized. "I looked at the clock and all of a sudden said, 'I have to go, I have to go!'"

Daddy shook his head. "It's okay," he said. "Your sister got nervous because she didn't want to be late to pick up the boys."

We fussed over the baby together. "*Che duce*, right, Daddy? He is so sweet, isn't he?" Daddy smiled as he agreed with me. I picked up John as he started to get fussy. I looked down at him and brought his cheek up to my lips. I gave him several tiny kisses on his cheek. He giggled. "This baby loves me!" I cooed. I looked over at Daddy and smiled. He had his head resting on the pillow. He looked so relaxed, just for a minute. It had been a long time since I had seen that tranquil look on my father's face.

"Daddy, do you remember when David was born? He was even smaller than this. I would put my doll's clothes on him and they would fit." Daddy nodded. He leaned on his side as he thought of that time.

"*Mi ricordo*," he said, remembering. "Your big, tough guy brother fainted at the hospital when he saw David for the first time. BOOM, he fell on the floor!" he said, slapping the mattress. Then his face turned red and he started to cough and laugh at the same time.

David was born in January, 1980. He was premature and it was said that he looked smaller than a roasting chicken from the supermarket. This little boy, my first nephew, was in the hospital for three months in an incubator before he was allowed to come home. Josephine cried every day. I was so anxious to see the baby, but I was too young to visit. The hospital would not allow children into the neo-natal unit. Then finally, at nine and a half years old, I held a baby in my arms for the first time.

Josephine taught me how to hold David. She sat beside me on her couch and instructed me how to hold his head and told me to be very gentle. She taught me how to give him his bottle without letting too much air get into his belly. Then she showed me how to put the baby on my shoulder and gently pat his back to help him burp. I always laughed when the baby burped in my ear, and Josephine would laugh too as she watched her baby sister taking care of her baby.

It took me a while to change his diaper. I had to watch Josephine a few times to get the hang of it. I teased her about the diapers, reminding her of the time I almost choked on a safety pin on her watch. "It's a good thing these things have tape instead of pins these days. I don't trust you around pins and babies!" She would give me a sarcastic face and wrinkle her nose at me. She would laugh about it too, though.

By the time Michael came along two years later, and then Jason four years after that, I was a pro. I would feed the kids, bathe them, even bake cakes with them, all the while pretending they were my babies and I was their mommy. I knew I had to be a mom one day. I felt it in my heart.

Now as I looked at Johnnie in my arms, I started humming a lullaby, the same one my mother sang to me when I was a baby. Softly, I sang to my godson. *"Ninna, ninna nanna, dormi baby, della Mamma. Ninna, ninna o, dormi baby, fai la vovo."* I put little Johnnie down on the bed beside Daddy. He fell asleep clutching my finger with his tiny hand. I stayed there beside him.

"Daddy, please tell me the story again, the one about when I was born." Daddy smiled as he looked over at the baby on the bed.

"Shh," he told me "Don't wake up the baby. When you were born it was a Saturday afternoon. When they brought you to the room where the babies were, the curtain was closed. Then the nurse came out of the door and said, 'Mr. John, we brought your baby girl to the nursery.'" Daddy was smiling. *"Lo sapevo, ho gridato,"* he said, telling me that in his heart he had had a feeling that I would be a girl. He just felt bad for Benny, who had wanted a brother. *"Povero Bernardo*, he wanted a brother so bad. Then the nurse opened up the curtain and before she even pointed out which pink blanket was holding my baby, I went to the window and hit my head on the glass. *La testa mi stavo rompere!"* That was it, my favorite part. I always loved to hear how Daddy was so elated on the day I was born that he almost broke his head on the glass window of the

146

nursery. He told me that he recognized me right away. "That is my *Americana*!" he said, pointing me out to the family members who had also been waiting for me to be born.

My cousin Carmen was at the hospital that day. It was her birthday too. "She was born just for me today, Zio. She was my birthday present this year!" Carmen was close to my parents. A year earlier, Mom and Dad baptized Carmen's youngest daughter, Angela. Carmen bragged to all of the other cousins, how the "baby" of the family was born on her birthday because she was just as special as her cousin Carmen.

I saw Daddy getting sleepy as we talked about the day I was born, and then I reminded him of my eighteenth birthday when my cousin and I celebrated together. The year I graduated high school, I went to Florida, where the family gave Carmen and me a joint birthday celebration. It was held at a restaurant owned by some of our relatives, including Carmen. Carmen and I sat side by side with matching cakes, one chocolate with white icing and the other white with chocolate frosting.

Although I missed my parents and family back home, this birthday celebration was so much fun. Zia Rosaria was there with her family. Then there was my godmother with most of her family, and Zia Adriana and Zio Filippo. Cousin Angela never forgets my birthday because it's the same day as her mother's.

I was taken out of my reminiscence when I heard the key turn in the door lock. I knew it was Josephine and prepared to be yelled at. I stayed in the bedroom with Daddy and didn't say a word.

Daddy may have been sick but I still felt safer in the room with him than alone with my sister when she was annoyed with me. Daddy knew my strategy and when Josephine walked in with a scowl on her face, Daddy's finger went right to his lip. "Shh," he warned Josephine. *"Il bambino sta dormire."* Daddy's vision may have been impaired but "the eyes" had not lost their touch. They still managed to get the message through to Josephine. With one look from Dad, Josephine picked up the baby and went into the living room. She managed to slap my leg on her way out and motion with her arm to follow her into the other room.

In the living room I explained to her why I had been late. She didn't care. She yelled at me in a whisper about how irresponsible that was, how she was depending on me.

I just nodded my head and kept saying, "Sorry Jo, sorry Jo."

Then she laughed and just dismissed me with a wave of her hand. "Well, forget it now," she said. "But I was almost late to pick up my kids!"

Again I said, "I'm sorry, Jo. I'm sorry." Now I was laughing. "Oh, now you don't love me anymore. Come on, my beautiful big sister who I love so much. Will you ever forgive me?"

Josephine gave me a dirty look with a big smile on her face. "Yeah, all right. You're lucky you said I was beautiful. That's the only reason I will forgive you." Without waking my godson I grabbed my sister's shoulders and kissed her roughly on both cheeks. She and the kids were laughing as they went next door to their apartment.

I went back into Daddy's bedroom to see if he had heard the exchange that just took place between his two daughters. I don't think he did because he was sound asleep. I left his door open so I could hear him in case he needed my help. Then I went to my own bedroom and left my door open too. As Daddy napped in his room, I lay down on my bed and thought again about the story he just told me about the day I was born.

Then someone else popped into my thoughts. My brother Benny. That poor little eight year-old kid who was waiting for a little brother. Maybe that's why Benny tortured me when I was a teenager. Whenever he saw me talking to a boy in the neighborhood, he would pull his car over to the curb, even in the middle of traffic. One time he saw me wearing those tight green pinstriped jeans Daddy hated. Right in front of my friend, he pulled me by the arm up the stoop and ordered me upstairs to change my pants. I was so humiliated. But now I get it. It was all about revenge for me being a girl instead of the brother he was waiting for. I laughed out loud. No, my big brother loves me. After all, I am his favorite. At least that is what I am content to believe!

By late April Daddy was walking around the house holding a portable oxygen tank and breathing with a tube in his nose. His hair had grown back, but it was completely white. The dark shiny waves were gone. He was so self-conscious about his thin frame that he wore a robe over his pajamas and clothes. Most of the time, he slept. The smell of food made him feel sick, so he ate next to nothing. I found myself keeping watch again outside my parents' bedroom, listening to Daddy breathe all through the night. What a way to remember the last year of being a teenager.

***

May, 1990

May 3, 1990 was Daddy's last birthday. He turned fifty-seven years old. What a difference a year can make in circumstances. In 1989 Francesca wanted to give Daddy a big birthday party because it would be the last year that she was living at home with us. She also brought up that Daddy never had a big birthday party and she wanted to do that for him. So we invited family and friends to the apartment and had plenty of food and drinks.

Francesca wrote Daddy a special poem and since I was the baby, I was chosen to recite it in front of everyone. I was fine up until the part about *me*, and then I choked up. My cousin Connie took over and read the rest of it.

Usually we would celebrate Daddy and Michael's birthdays together, since their birthdays were only a few days apart. Michael is Josephine's second son, and has had attitude since he was a baby. He was a tough little guy and he had a thing for the ladies even when he was a toddler. Daddy would hold Michael on his lap and every time there were women on television in swimsuits or low cut gowns, Daddy would point them out to Michael, saying "Michael, you see over there, look, ball-ee, ball-ee!" and then Daddy would laugh out loud as he lovingly made a ladies' man out of his grandson.

Michael would then do the same thing to Daddy. "Nonno, look! Ball-ee, ball-ee!" he'd coo, as they admired the breasts of the sexy women on television. The whole family would laugh and Michael's face would turn red. He had that Irish complexion like his Dad's, so when he blushed he would turn a rosy color.

This year, though, we had Michael's cake on a different day. Daddy's party got funny and fast. Daddy and his best friend, Zio Filippo, of course indulged in I don't recall what drink of choice that evening. Apparently whatever they were drinking made them feel mighty jolly. As the evening went on, the music got louder and we kids convinced Zio and Daddy to get up and dance. It was so funny. The two friends started dancing and tried to get the women into it but Zia Adriana and Mom, laughing so hard, were waving them off. So the men were dancing and we were all cheering them on.

They were teasing their wives and pretending they were going to take off their clothes, pulling at their sweaters and shaking their hips. Again, Zia and Mom were turning away from their husbands with tears on their blushing faces, laughing so hard. The rest of us were also in hysterics by then. Antoinette was videotaping the whole scene and you could hear her voice, "Uh oh, divorce court this week!" joking about how Mom and Zia Adriana would surely make their husbands pay for being so silly that evening and for drinking too much.

We had a great night. That was almost twenty years ago now and our two families still talk about that evening and how much fun we all had. A big difference from the birthday Daddy would have just one year later. On Daddy's birthday in 1990, our family, the married kids and their families, were present. There were so many people, but it was quiet. By then, Daddy had become so thin and frail that none of his clothes fit him anymore. Just wearing regular clothing was uncomfortable to him, and he would be in pajamas and a robe all the time now. He could not breathe without the assistance of the oxygen tank, so he always had a tube in his nose.

In the last family pictures in which Dad is still present, Daddy is not able to stand up steadily, so he is seated in his chair and the rest of us are gathered around him. You see him forcing a smile on his thin face. The rest of us look pale and tired, kneeling or standing beside him.

We took a photograph of Mom and all of us kids around Dad. Being the only daughter-in-law, Ben's wife took a picture sitting beside Dad on the armrest of his chair. Then we took a photograph of Daddy with his sons-in-law. Since Joey and I were not married yet, he didn't get up when my sisters' husbands did. But then, just before the picture was shot, Daddy put up his hand and said *"No, aspetta, dov'è Joe di Susie?"* asking where *my* Joey was.

So then everyone said, "That's right! Where's the baby brother-in-law? Get in the picture, Joey." Mom and I exchanged looks and both of us were about to cry. We turned our faces and took a deep breath. My Joey, back in our family, and Daddy's gesture made it official. My brothers-in-law took turns patting Joey on the back, teasing him as if he were now the "new guy" on a team. Joey had a big smile on his face when he looked at me and winked. That was it, the last of the festivities in our home that year.

***

Godsister

Daddy's health got progressively worse right after his birthday. My heart broke a little more each day. That stupid tube in his nose and around his ears all the time. His head had shrunk to the size of a small cantaloupe. His cheeks were drawn and his face was pale and dry. That beautiful olive complexion and strong cheekbones were

151

only a memory. Daddy looked like an old man now.

I barely left the house, except to go to work. I had no choice but to go to work because apart from Daddy's social security disability, which had just been approved, my wages were the only steady income we had in the house. Thank goodness the other kids helped out too. Mom had enough to worry about.

One quiet day when I was home with Mom and Dad, the three of us got a big surprise. Mom and Dad's godchild, Angela came from Florida to visit us. Angela is the youngest daughter of my cousin Carmen, with whom I share my birthday. Because she is only a year older than I, the two of us grew up very close. Then, when she was in the seventh grade, her family moved to Long Island. The distance between us increased when she went away to boarding school. After that, she lived upstate for a bit with some of our cousins, and by the time she paid us this visit, she had moved to Florida with her mom.

Angela and I always stayed in touch, so she was aware that Daddy's health was getting worse. The thought of not saying goodbye to Daddy was unbearable to her and she knew she had to make the trip. Luckily, she had a friend in Florida who was a student at pilot school, and he volunteered to give Angela a ride to New York by helicopter. It was a brave thing to do, but she had great motivation. Angela not only wanted to see Daddy but she also wanted to make sure that *I* was okay. We had been talking on the phone during Dad's illness and she could hear the strain in my voice. She did not trust me to tell her the entire truth, so she came to check on me in person.

Angela and I were so close growing up that we considered ourselves far more than cousins. We joked how we were "Godsisters." This was a rank that had to be much closer than cousins or even good friends. We had a bond that no one could question.

Angela's parents, Carmen and Richie, had divorced when Angela was young. Despite the divorce, though, Richie remained a part of our family and was particularly close to Daddy. Richie and Carmen were younger and more liberal than Daddy. (*Most people* were more liberal than Dad.) Carmen and Richie had different rules for Angela than my parents had for me. I was not allowed out very often, and Angela was. As little girls, we lived on opposite ends of the same block for a while. Daddy said I was not allowed to walk to Angela's house by myself because it was not safe for a little girl to walk that distance alone. Angela would get annoyed with Daddy, but more than that, she felt sorry for me. My father was so strict and it was hard for her to understand Daddy's whole mentality about his youngest daughter.

Angela used to come to my house equipped with supplies for our time together. She would pack a big cardboard box with her dolls and doll clothing, and sometimes she brought games or other toys. She would drag that box all the way up the block to my apartment building and carry it up three flights of stairs so that the two of us could play together. In elementary school the two of us would walk home together. In sixth grade, her last year in the same school, a new boy was in our class. He had brown hair and really nice eyes. Angela had a crush on him. He liked Angela too, as many of the boys did. Why not? She was always really pretty and never shy. I was the girl all the guys thought was pretty but "liked as their friend." I was the girl they called when they needed help with their homework, or if they had a secret to tell and didn't trust anyone else to keep it.

I didn't mind Angela getting the attention and I enjoyed going along for the ride. I always got in trouble, though, because I would get home late from school. We would pass the boy's house and sometimes see his mother outside. We would stop and talk to her for a little while and Signora Giulia was always so sweet to us. The mother she really liked Angela, and she liked that I spoke Italian. I was usually too shy to speak Italian, though, because most people in the neighborhood spoke the Sicilian dialect and I didn't.

In our house we spoke Italian. In Tripoli, the Italians who had migrated there did not speak the Sicilian dialect of their native towns. They all spoke to each other in standard Italian. That is what my parents had gotten accustomed to, and that's how they spoke to us. Daddy saved the Sicilian for his friends. For instance, at the barber shop, Dad would chat with Mr. Charlie and the other *paesani* who were waiting for haircuts, in Sicilian.

Our neighborhood was made up mostly of Italians and Germans when I was growing up. Among the Italian community though, everyone knew everyone else. And if they didn't know you personally, they knew your business. The good part was that everyone looked out for everyone else's children. When the Italian men Daddy's age saw me even a short distance from a local café, Daddy knew about it. One time, one of my older cousins had me go through the back entrance of a café because she knew a guy there who had offered the two of us ice cream. My cousin was older than I and was in charge of walking me home that day, which left me no choice but to follow her inside. It was really harmless and we were only there for the time it took for this boy to scoop up two ice cream cones. But apparently one of Daddy's *paesani* told him that I was there that day.

That night when Daddy came home he did not answer me when I greeted him. He only gave me his cheek and accepted my kiss. My mother looked at him strangely but did not question him. We got through dinner without Daddy speaking to me. As I got up to help Mom clear the dishes he put out his hand, and told me, *"Tu non ti muovere,"* advising me that is was best I didn't move. Mom went into the kitchen. I could see her by the sink trying to listen.

He very calmly told me that if I *ever* walked into a café again I would get such a slap across the face that I would feel the sting for weeks after. He even made the motion close to my face without actually striking me. Tears came to my eyes but I would not cry. I lifted my head up in defiance and did not even try to explain what had happened. I got up from the table and started to walk toward my room before the tears could make their way down my cheeks. Daddy called to me, and asked if I understood his warning, *"Hai capito, signorina?!"*

If you come from outside this culture or are not familiar with it, you may wonder what the big deal was. It has to do with appearances and what "people will say." A young woman who goes into a place frequented mostly by men opens herself up to being talked about. It can actually ruin a nice girl's reputation, and once that is lost it cannot be regained. The woman doesn't have to be doing anything -- it is enough that it *looks* like she might be doing something. To Americans, this seems like much ado about nothing, but in *my* old neighborhood, it was serious business!

Now, as a grown woman, *married* to a Sicilian man, I keep my eyes down and walk quickly every time I pass a café where men are standing outside. If my husband is with me he laughs, noticing my head down and the quickness in my steps. "What's the matter, Sue?" he'll say, "you still thinking of your father?" I look at my husband and smile.

"Yes," I chuckle. "Knowing my father, he'll have something drop on my head if I look in that direction!" My husband will pat me on the back as if he agrees with my father and his old school mentality.

Angela and I talked about that story and others like it during the few days she stayed with us. One afternoon, as Daddy slept in the next room, Angela and I lay on my bed staring up at the ceiling. Angela too, was listening to the labored sound of Daddy's breathing. She turned to me and with tears in her eyes, said, "You know, Sue, your father loves me so much."

I sat up, a little confused about what she saying. "Of course my father loves you, Ang, you are his godchild." She shook her head.

"No, Susie, I mean he *really* loves me. When we were kids, you could never go out or you had to be home really early." I kept listening. "Remember that time you were graduating from high school? I was nineteen and you were almost eighteen. It was two years ago, remember? I came in from Long Island and slept here in your house. There was a beach party that weekend at Rockaway."

I nodded my head remembering what she was talking about. "You were so pissed off at him that weekend Ang," I said, grinning. "'How can you live like this?!'" you asked me.

Angela looked at me and suddenly tears were rolling down her cheeks. "That's what I'm talking about, Sue. He yelled at me that time because you came home at eleven o'clock and I stayed out later without you. I thought it was so ridiculous that time that I was nineteen and you were almost eighteen, and he told us to be home at eleven o'clock on a Saturday night!"

I laughed as I wiped the tears with a tissue from my cousin's face. I kissed her pretty cheek. "I know, Ang. The next day I had to work at six o'clock in the morning and I got a lecture from my father about you. *I* got in trouble for not bringing you home when *I* came home."

During my senior year of high school I worked at a bakery around the corner from our building. On weekends I had to open the store at 6:00 a.m. It was still dark at that hour, so even though I was seventeen years old, Daddy would walk me to the bakery every Saturday and Sunday morning. He would get out of bed and just put a jacket over his pajamas and walk me around the corner in his slippers. He would help me get the gate and door open, then wait until I was inside the store with the lights on and the doors locked before he left. By that time a couple of the workers would have arrived and he'd feel better about leaving.

The weekend that Angela was recalling, Daddy scolded me on the way to the bakery. "*Perchè?*" he asked me, "*perchè sei venuta in casa ieri sera senza la tua cugina?!*" reprimanding me for coming home the night before without my cousin.

"*Papà,*" I answered shakily, "I can't tell Angela what to do. She's nineteen years old. I told her you wanted us home by eleven o'clock and she thought that was crazy. I told her you would get mad if we were late and I told her I had to leave because I had work this morning anyway. I couldn't force her to come home with me. I came home when I was supposed to."

Daddy was not impressed. "I know how you are by now. Maybe Angela doesn't!" I told him. Daddy gave me "the eyes," so I kept my mouth shut after that.

Daddy dropped the subject with me but gave Angela the cold shoulder when she woke up that morning. The two of them had had it out already when Angela got home the night before. Just as he would with his own children, he had stayed up late waiting for Angela to get home that night. Angela was not even that late, but it didn't matter, — it was still past a given curfew. And that was a clear sign of disrespect, at least according to my father. It was unacceptable behavior for his own children and for his godchild as well. Angela defended herself.

"*Zio,*" she said, "how can you tell me it's too late to come home? My mother doesn't tell me to come home at eleven o'clock on a Saturday! Don't you think that is a little ridiculous? I am not a baby. And Susie is almost eighteen! That's too early for her too to come home from a party."

Ang told me that Daddy's face was so red as she spoke. She said he cleared his throat when she mentioned my name. I could picture his exact coloring at that moment. There was a certain shade of SICILIAN RED that Daddy's face would turn when he was really angry.

I was trying to listen from my bedroom but could not hear that well, so I tiptoed closer in the foyer. I was praying silently that the old floor wouldn't creak under my feet. The last thing I wanted was to get called into the conversation. *Thank you, floor,* I thought when my eavesdropping went unnoticed. After all, Angela would be going back to her mother's house in Long Island when this confrontation was over. I had to *live* with this man! It was his way and no other way. At almost eighteen I was already well aware of that. Remember Ben and the fake fainting.

Daddy took a deep breath and tried to be calm when speaking to his godchild. Then he answered her. "*Senti,* Angela," he said, asking her to pay attention. "I love you, *sei mia figlioccia,*" he said, reminding her of their relationship. "But when you stay in *my* house, you follow *my* rules. I am not your mother or your father. I know that. But your mother *and* your father, they trust me when you stay here. You can stay with Susie any time you want. *But* when my *daughter* comes home when she is supposed to, *you* better come home too. Otherwise you can't stay here anymore! *Mi dispiace,* I'm sorry, if you don't like that!"

Thankfully, Angela knew better than to continue the argument. She came into my room, unaware that I had been listening the whole time. She plopped on my bed and cried. "How do you live like this?! He is so ridiculous!"

I shook my head as I patted Angela's hand. "I'm just used to it, Godsister! That's just how he is. I told you but you didn't believe me."

Without even changing our clothes we stared up at the ceiling that night too. The next day when I got home from work we went up on the roof to take in some sun. Angela then retold the whole story to my sister Fran. Fran confirmed what I had already told Ang the night before. "That's my father, Angela. It's his way and that's it!"

***

Rue, Bue, Lue, and Sue

During the couple of days that Angela stayed with us we had time to reminisce about the old times when we were kids. Angela remembered one of the few nights I was allowed to sleep at her house. Her mother, Carmen, had to call Daddy and practically swear on her life that she would not leave us alone for a minute. You would think I was going to some faraway place — they only lived up the block at the time.

Finally Daddy agreed, and so we had our pajama party. We played loud music and danced around in our pajamas. We put on the soundtracks of "Grease" and "The Sound of Music" and pretended we were the characters from these movies.

When Angela's sister Maria was in seventh grade in our Catholic school, the class put on a production of "The Sound of Music." Maria played one of the nuns at the abbey. There is a scene in the play in which all the nuns are looking high and low for the Julie Andrews character, Maria. They are calling, "Maria, Maria, Maria!" That night, we were teasing Maria about her very Queens accent, calling out, "MARIA!" louder than all of the other girls in her class. We were laughing so hard and Maria was throwing pillows at us.

That night, Carmen made us a special pudding treat. She was kind enough to let us help and as a result, the pudding it didn't turn out as pretty as it was in the TV commercial. It was supposed to be Cool Whip and Jell-O Pudding in alternating layers of vanilla pudding, then whipped cream, then chocolate pudding, and then more whipped cream on top. Instead, our version came out like a big transparent glass of creamy cappuccino, because everything just kind of melted together, forming a light brownish mass of sweetness. It didn't come out as planned but it sure tasted delicious!

Tara, Angela, Lisa, and I were always together as kids. Maria was a few years older than we were so she had older friends or hung around with our older cousins. When Maria got married, the rest of us were in her bridal party.

Tara, Angela, Lisa, and I were together so much we came up with a nickname for ourselves. We would say, "Rue, Bue, Lue, and Sue, True Cousins Forever!" Then shake on it. We'd promised to always be there for the others, should they need us. And I needed them now, that was for sure.

The nickname was derived from our first names shortened and combined. Tara's mom Sylvia had given her an American name at a time when everyone else was, Maria, Josephine, Joey, Tony, etc. The aunts, uncles, and Tara's own grandmother, had trouble saying just

"Tara." At times they affectionately called her *Taruzza*! We teased her about it and started calling her *Rue* for short.

Bue, came out of the family teasing Angela, calling her *Angelina Buffalina*, which was just a playful way of saying her name. And Lisa's *Lue* came from Zia Adriana's daughters, who one day were just teasing Lisa, calling her *Louisiana Purchase* or something like that. Lisa told me the story once but I don't remember it. That turned into her nickname *Lue* and there you have, *Rue, Bue, Lue*, and me of course, *Sue*!

We would write that on our letters to each other when Angela was in boarding school. Then when Tara and Lisa moved upstate we still used it on our correspondence to each other.

Before Tara and Lisa moved, they were living in a two-family house two blocks away from me. Even though I was a teenager, Daddy still wanted me to have a chaperone to walk me back and forth to their house. My "chaperones" were Joey and Steven, Lisa's brothers. Steven was my age, even four months younger than I am, and Joey was at least four years older than I. But still, they were BOYS and I was a girl, so they qualified and gladly took on the job of my "bodyguards."

Steven and I were in the same class during most of our years of Catholic school. The guys, as with Fran and Benny, thought of me as "Steve's cousin," so they always treated me with respect. Most of Steven's best friends became my best friends too, because we were always together.

During all my years of Catholic school not only did I have my cousin and our friends, but I had the same best friend from my first day of first grade until and beyond graduation from eighth grade. Like Steven who moved on to a Catholic high school so did my friend Ann Marie. My Annie.

Annie and I had both been accepted at the same all-girls private school, only my parents could not afford the tuition. I remember being so upset that we would not be together for high school.

Despite going to separate schools, though, Annie and I kept in touch. We remained very close through high school and Annie's time in college. I remember feeling so excited when Annie graduated and became a CPA. She always worked so hard and I was so proud of her.

It was a little scary as a teenager moving on to another school without Steven and without Annie. When I came in as a freshman, Steven's older brother, Joey, was a senior and he took over the *job* of looking after me. For the first week, he and his girlfriend walked me to every single class, every single period. Joey wanted to make sure everyone knew I was his little cousin and they better not bother me. He also wanted me to feel calmer and safer because it was such a big school, so different from our little private Catholic school that I was used to.

Luckily, it did not take long for me to adjust. I knew most of the Italian kids already because we came from the same neighborhood. Some of my friends from Catholic school were also attending the same high school. Mostly I just went from class to class, minding my own business and doing all my work, until I got a social life.

Since I was not allowed to stay out late on the weekends, or even go out during the week, I started cutting classes during the spring of my freshman year. It was the only time I got to be with my friends. Many of my friends' parents worked too, so sometimes we went to someone's empty house. Other times, we left the neighborhood completely, with our friends who were old enough to have cars. I never told my cousin Joey or his sister Lisa, who went to the same school. I didn't want them to yell at me. But they found out later when the "cut cards" were going to their address instead of mine. Their mother, my cousin Josephine, pulled me aside and very gently told me she would not tell my mother, *this time*, but would have to tell if she got any more cards.

It was because of my Italian teacher, Mr. Pulera, my mother found out about my cutting class. He called my mom when he noticed a pattern in my absences. I was grounded by Mom for a whole marking period. She threatened to tell Daddy if she got any more phone calls. Thanks to my cousin Josephine, my Italian teacher, and my mom, I did not fail and become a dropout.

My brother Ben, who was a salesman at the time for a plumbing supply company, heard about what happened. His office was in the area, so he would pass the school at different times of the day to make sure I was inside and not outside.

Once when a teacher was absent and we had a sub, I stepped outside during one period to grab a bite to eat. Ben caught me walking out of the deli and got out of his car. He opened up the door on the passenger side and had me get in. He drove me right up to the front entrance of the school and watched as I walked up the stairs. He waved to me as I turned to look at him from the doorway of the school. He smiled and motioned for me to keep walking. I cursed him under my breath all the way up the stairs back to my classroom.

My cousin Josephine is the first of Orazio and Giuseppa's twenty-five grandchildren. I am the youngest. Because of the age difference, it was natural for Josephine to treat me more like a niece than a cousin. Two of her children were older than I. She always thought to include me in the various activities with her kids. She took me to see my first movie in a theatre, "STAR WARS." There were so many of us kids piled in her car that day, but we never minded being squashed as long as we were together.

When the teenage singing group, Menudo, first became popular in the eighties, Josephine bought tickets for her daughter Lisa, and took the rest of us along as well. This is a special memory for me because even our friends Grace and Margaret joined us, with their mother, Signora Francesca. It was also the first live concert I had ever been to. I love my cousin Josephine. She has been a role model for me because of her generosity and good nature. Josephine has always been a great mom, a working mom, like me. She always made time for her kids, even when there really was so little. Not just for her own kids, but for her nieces and nephews, and even for me.

Daddy would be amused on those mornings when he would watch from the bedroom window as Josephine ran to the train station. She was always late because she had to get three kids ready for school before heading into Manhattan to work. Daddy would come into the living room chuckling, and would tell Mom and me, *"Ho visto mia nipote Pina correre per il treno!"* as he described her running for the train.

Even when Josephine and her sisters, Angela and Sylvia, moved upstate, Josephine would always convince Dad to let me go there for the weekend, and would promise to get me back in time for school on Monday. During the summer, I would spend a week at a time in Middletown with my cousins.

That was my first introduction to suburban life. My cousins had huge three-bedroom houses with a downstairs *and* an upstairs. They had a front yard and a backyard, too. They had driveways and basements. It would feel strangely pleasant when I came back to my three-bedroom apartment on the fourth floor. Somehow, that is what I was most comfortable with. I always knew I was close to home when, getting off the Thruway, I'd see graffiti on walls. Even the air smelled different, that familiar smell of the city air.

When Angela and my other cousins moved to the suburbs of Long Island and Upstate New York, I spent the rest of my childhood in Queens. Having Angela at home with me those few days in May brought back so many memories. I longed for the days of my childhood when everything seemed okay, when everyone who loved me was working so hard to protect me from getting hurt. All I had to think about was going to school, doing homework, and what to wear to the roller skating rink on the weekends (that is, when my cousins convinced Daddy to let me go), or if a boy would ask me to dance at one of the church dances at our Catholic school.

During the time of Daddy's illness, Tara was still living upstate with her mom. Tara and Sylvia had come down to visit our family, too. Sometimes Steven and I spoke on the phone, and neither one of us would ever want to end the conversation. We said goodbye at least ten times before one of us would finally hang up. I wished at the time that I could get together with all those with whom I shared my childhood and put my arms around them for one big hug. How it would have helped ease some of the pain I felt as I watched Daddy slip out of my life. I was desperately trying to hold on to my childhood and desperately trying to hold on to my father.

When Angela left, she gave me a half of a gold charm – a heart split in two. She kept one half and I had the other. She said it would keep us together in our hearts and that I should wear it during this time that I needed her most. I wore it on a chain for a long time after she left, touching it now and again in the days that followed. I would think about all the memories we had exchanged during her visit.

Sometimes I would wish that gold charm was a kind of magic lamp that would bring me back to those days. I would envision myself a kid sharing French fries with my cousins upstate on one of our midnight runs to McDonalds, or recreating *Grease* in Angela's living room during our sleepover. Ironically, I still was a kid, just nineteen years old. In a couple of months I would be twenty, but I felt so much older.

***

The Last Week...

On Memorial Day that year I just wanted to stay home and do nothing, but Dad would not hear of it. My boyfriend's parents had invited me over to their home for a barbecue. Daddy insisted that Joey and I spend the time with Joey's family and just enjoy the day. He reassured me that he was fine and that he and Mom would not be alone. Maria and Joe were going there and Fran and her husband would pass by as well. My sister Josephine practically lived in our apartment in those days.

I don't remember the details of that afternoon at all anymore. I can only remember the details of that evening and how that night, my life changed forever. It was the day my childhood was officially over and I became an adult.

That night I had Joey take me home pretty early. I was really tired and just wanted to relax and watch television with my parents for the rest of the evening. I asked Joey if he would mind just dropping me off. He understood and went home to spend the rest of the evening with his family too.

By the time I got home, everyone who had visited had already left. I found Daddy lying on the couch. He had a sheet under his body and a pillow under his small head. When I walked in the door he looked at me and tried to smile but it looked more like a wince, as though he were very uncomfortable. "Everyone left?" I asked my mother.

She turned to me and said, *"Tuo padre non si sente bene,"* telling me how Dad was not feeling well. I sat on the coffee table beside the couch and took Daddy's hand. Even that made him wince. I put his hand back on his belly. "You okay, Daddy?" I asked him. He did not answer me with words. He only shook his head. He tried to sit up on his side to see me better, he couldn't. "It's okay, *Papà, stai.* Stay, relax."

"Aiutami. Aiutami che non mi posso nianche muovere," he said, almost in a whisper. Daddy was asking for help because he couldn't move anymore.

Mom came into the living room and asked me what happened. *"Che c'è, cosa ti sta dire?"* she asked, wanting to know what he had said. I told Mom that Daddy could not move anymore.

"Should I call an ambulance?" I asked. Daddy managed to reach my hand and when I looked at him. Even as sick as he was, he gave me "the eyes," and so I knew that meant *no*.

"Voglio andare a letto," he said, quietly agitated. "I want to go to my

bed, I need help," he told Mommy and me, holding his hands as far up into the air as he could. Mom and I exchanged looks and I stood up. We tried to pull Daddy up to sit but Mom let out a moan of pain as she held one hand on her back. Daddy waved her away. "No, don't hurt yourself," he told her. Daddy looked at me.

"It's okay, Mommy," I said, "Stay there. I'll help Daddy." But Daddy could not budge. Suddenly the pain and the illness just overwhelmed him. His body was lifeless. He could barely even speak. There I stood, nineteen years old, five foot three. I felt so small as I looked down at Daddy's frail body and thought, *You have to do this. Please, God, help me to help him, please.*

I put one arm under Daddy's arms and the other under his knees. I took a deep breath as I lifted him. Closing my eyes for a second, I heard Mom gasp. Daddy was not even that heavy but he was much taller than I was. I started to carry him into the bedroom and Mommy followed. As my face turned red, Mom grabbed Daddy's legs, which still left me with most of his weight. We got to the edge of the bed and I laid Daddy down on the side nearest to the door. Then Mom and I adjusted his body to make him more comfortable.

Daddy had his eyes on me the whole time I was carrying him into his room. I kept my gaze fixed on his, as if his eyes would bring me strength. I felt the heat in my flushed face. It was the end of May, a warm evening, and with the lifting and carrying, sweat dripped from my forehead and was stinging my eyes.

Daddy managed to touch my hand, so I turned to look at him. He did not say a word and somehow found the strength to give me a half smile as he cringed, trying to find a comfortable position. I had to leave the room. I touched his foot gently and forced a smile back at him.

I walked into the bathroom and locked the door. Turning the faucet on, I splashed cold water on my face and cried. I left the water running so my parents would not hear me. A moment later Mom was knocking on the door. I took a deep breath and splashed water on my face again. I held the towel to my face as I opened the door slowly. I looked at Mom and tears came to my eyes. Mom put her arms around me, but I held my crying this time. So did my mother. Neither of us wanted Daddy to hear us. Mom kissed my face and whispered in my ear, *"Grazie, Gioia mia, grazie."* She was grateful for what I had done.

Before returning to the bedroom, Mom said, "Call your sister. Tell Josephine to call the doctor right away from her house. You call your brother and your sisters and tell them to come over."

The doctor who was taking care of Daddy was a friend with whom Daddy sometimes socialized at the hospital. He loved Daddy. When Daddy had become too ill to go the doctor's office, the doctor came to our home. So when Josephine called him that Monday evening, he came right away, and so did the rest of the family. Not only my siblings, but my aunts and uncles also rushed over. Before the end of that night, our house was full of people. The vigil at Daddy's bedside had begun, Memorial Day, 1990.

In the days that followed, the house was full all the time. My aunts came over in the daytime then returned in the evening with my uncles. My cousins were in and out all day. As people came and went, they brought us food. Zia Rosaria came up from Florida to be with her dying brother-in-law.

Mom had told her sister about how I carried Daddy in my arms into the bedroom. One afternoon when Zia was there, I walked into the kitchen as she stood by the sink. I sat at the kitchen table as I heard the tail end of Mom and Zia's conversation. It brought tears to my eyes again as I remembered the experience. I put my head down on the table, too tired to cry. Zia Rosaria stood behind me and rubbed my shoulders. I reached up and squeezed Zia's hand without looking up at her.

My cousin Yola and her twin sister Yvana were there that afternoon. Yola said to Zia Rosaria, "Ma, why don't you give her a drink?

Something light just to help her relax a little bit." Zia Rosaria went to the liquor cabinet and picked up a bottle of dry vermouth. Yola took a glass from the counter and filled it with ice. Zia Rosaria opened up the fridge and took out a lemon. She cut a wedge and dropped it into the glass. Yola filled the glass with the vermouth. It's amazing how they knew exactly what to do. I picked up the glass and drank half of it down in one gulp. I felt the warmth go to my cheeks right away. Then I put my head down on the table again. Zia Rosaria stood behind me, still rubbing my shoulders.

The next day was the same. Everyone in and out of the apartment all day long, checking on Daddy. Zia Rosaria's kids, Manny and Josephine, also came up from Florida. They too, wanted to see Daddy. Everyone was coming over every day. There was a steady stream of aunts, uncles, and cousins. Some of my friends even came over. They would be crying as they left Daddy's room, calling to mind all the times he had been so nice to them.

I would not leave Daddy's side. I sat beside him on the bed with my legs crossed, as a child does when you tell them "sit like a pretzel." I sat that way for hours at a time. When the pain would start in my leg, tiny tears would fall down my cheeks until my legs just got numb. I was not moving.

One day that week a friend of Daddy's named Josephine, came by. Josephine and Daddy had worked together for many years in the hospital dietary department and they had become good friends. Josephine tells me now that Daddy was the best friend she ever had. Josephine had a nice family — a husband and two sons, Peter and Paul. Daddy had been very close not only to Josephine, but to her sons as well. The two young men liked Daddy and always treated him respectfully. Daddy thought very highly of these two boys.

The day Josephine came to see Daddy, she sat in a chair right beside him. He was not really talking anymore. He was taking Demeral for the pain and was unconscious most of the time.

Suddenly Daddy opened his eyes and smiled. He turned his head and looked at Josephine. "Hey, Johnnie," she greeted him. She took his hand. Daddy smiled at Josephine.

"Josie," he said, "I just saw Paul. He was okay. He looks good, Josie."

Josephine bit her lip, as did the rest of us. Josephine's son Paul had died unexpectedly at a very young age. He went to work one day and had a brain aneurism. Josephine, her husband, and their son Peter were devastated. Anyone who knew their family had taken it badly. Paul was a very well-liked young man. Daddy loved Paul and had been so saddened by his death. He still had a good relationship with Josephine's other son, Peter. Less than a year before, Mom and Dad had been guests at Peter's wedding and Daddy had been so happy for Peter.

While everyone else called Daddy either "John" or "Battista," Josephine always called him "Johnnie." He always called Josephine "Josie." Whenever Josephine got a ride from someone at work, she always made sure Daddy was dropped off too. Whenever one of us went to pick Daddy up from work, we always dropped Josephine off at home, too. Josephine and her family had become good friends of our family. They were exactly what people mean when they use the phrase "good people."

Josephine looked at Daddy and smiled. She shook his hand gently, "Oh yeah, Johnnie, you saw my Paul?"

"I saw Paul, Josie. I saw Paul," he said. Then he closed his eyes again. Josephine held on to Daddy's hand a minute longer as a tear rolled down her cheek. Mom went to my room and closed the door. She was crying.

There was another time that day that Daddy spoke again. I was seated beside him on the bed as I had been all along. Daddy opened his eyes and noticed me watching him. He smiled and lifted his hand up to my face. With the back of his hand he caressed my cheek. "*Silvana, che sei bella,*" he said. Then he closed his eyes again. Daddy had mistaken me for my mother. As he touched my face he told "me" how pretty I was. I sat there smiling as I held Daddy's hand on my face. I did not want to let go. EVER.

Someone had gone into the kitchen to tell Mommy what just happened, so she came right into the bedroom. She asked the rest of us to leave the room, saying she wanted to be alone with her husband for a little while. As I got up, I found that my legs had turned to jelly. One of my cousins grabbed me and helped me stand up. I shook out my legs until I got them steady again.

Everyone else went into the living room or the kitchen. I went to my bedroom to check what I looked like. What a disaster. My face was pale, my hair looked like a big frizz ball. *Did I shower this morning?* I thought. Maybe now is a good time, while things are quiet. I grabbed a robe and a towel and headed for the bathroom.

As I walked down the hall, I turned back, wanting to look in on my parents first. The door was open and I could not help but look at the two of them. The picture of my parents on my father's death bed. I got the chills.

Mom had managed to sit on the edge of the bed and was able to lay Daddy's head upon her chest. I just stared at them a moment, as neither of them said anything. I was thinking how Daddy had just thought he was looking at Mom when she was younger. How he loved my mother. She was so young when he fell in love with her.

I remember Mom telling me her own stories of her courtship with Daddy. She was only fifteen when they were engaged. She was a child. She would wash the family's laundry in the courtyard on the side closest to Daddy's apartment door. As she noticed him walking home from work through the gate, she would sing songs of two young people admiring one another from afar and dreaming of the day they would be together. As Daddy got closer he would look at her from the corner of his eye, she told me, and Mom would turn around and pretend she didn't see him at all.

Mom told me how Nonna Maria "put her to the test" before she and Daddy were married. Nonna had to go to the hospital because Zia Giuseppina was ailing with kidney stones. Mom was at Nonna's house already, so Nonna gave her instructions. She told her, "Okay, *signorina, sei pronta per sposarti a mio figlio, vediamo se sei capasce di cucinare.*" Nonna Maria challenged the teenage Silvana, saying that if the young girl was ready to marry her son, she had better know how to cook.

All the ingredients for a meat sauce and pasta were in the kitchen. Pots and pans on the stove and everything. "When we have our dinner this evening, we'll see if you are ready to marry my son," she said. And she left Silvana by herself to cook dinner for the whole family.

Luckily, Nonna Giuseppa had taught Mom how to cook when Mom was a child. Before Mom could work she would cook at home so that Nonna and Zia Carmela would not have to do it when they came home tired. But despite her abilities, Mom was still a nervous wreck that day.

When Daddy's family sat down at the table that evening, everyone devoured Mom's food, some of them even licking the sauce from their fingers. Nonna Maria said nothing until everyone had finished. Daddy was eating with pleasure and had a big grin on his face. He ate every last bit on his plate. I remember Mom blushing when she would tell me that detail of the story.

As Mommy got up to start clearing the dishes, Nonna Maria, patted her hand. Mom looked at her future mother-in-law and waited for her comment. Nonna Maria cracked a smile, "*Brava, figia mia, brava!*" giving her blessing and confirming that Mom was ready to marry my father.

I smiled in spite of the incredible sadness I suddenly felt. Mom was his Silva, and he was her Batti. Mom wears a golden heart on a necklace around her neck. It has a little ruby in the center. The engraving on it reads *Batte per te*. It was one of the first gifts Daddy ever gave Mom, which was a symbol that "his heart was beating for her."

When Mom worked in Manhattan, she almost got mugged as she waited for the train one day. A man tried to grab that same necklace right from Mom's neck. Mom grabbed the heart and chain with one hand and punched the man hard, right in the face, with the other hand. The young man got scared of a tough Italian Mom and ran away. He ran so fast, he was never caught by good citizens who tried to grab him until they could find a cop.

We teased Mom for days, as Daddy called her "Rocky." Mom would laugh and say all the time, "Nobody is taking this heart away from me!" Daddy would pat her hand and smile at his wife. Daddy knew Mom was crazy about him. Crazy enough to risk her life to hold on to a gift that Daddy gave her. A heart that she treasured.

Then we kids would join Daddy laughing and chanting, "Go, Mommy! Go, Rocky!"

Mommy would slap Daddy's leg and motion with *her* eyes to shut us up now. "*Okay, basta!*" Daddy would tell us. "Please, that's enough, or else I have to sleep on the couch tonight!"

Daddy's face would turn red as he roared with laughter. Mom would roll her eyes at him and slap his leg again. The rest of us would follow our father as he teased Mom. Mom would laugh too, in spite of herself.

Look at them, look at them now. Mom had put up a fight, even now. She had not left Daddy's side and had encouraged him every day that it would be okay, even when she knew Dad realized it would not be. He had wanted the truth from his doctors, the real prognosis, and they gave it to him.

Mom took Daddy's hands that held her own and brought them up to her lips. "*Ti voglio tanto bene, Battista. Ti amo,*" she said, proclaiming her love for him. Daddy could not answer Mom. The words remained in his heart at that moment. But he did pull back his hand and gently kissed Mom's hands this time. He held her hands gently against his face. There were tears on my mother's face but a smile across her lips. She looked up and noticed me watching as the tears rolled down my cheeks as well.

"I'm sorry," I mouthed to her without saying it aloud. She shook her head and smiled at me, showing me that is was okay.

I was suddenly ashamed of myself for intruding on my parents' intimate moment. I turned around and went into the bathroom. I took a hot shower and just let the water run on my head, already feeling like I was drowning.

Once I was showered and dressed I reclaimed my post beside Daddy. I looked around the room and saw so many faces. We were all there together, just like at Fran's wedding, when we put our arms around one another and sang *Ti Amo*.

That day in that room, no one was singing but we were still together, still saying, without words, *Ti amo*, telling my father we loved him. Our family had come together to be with him the final hours of his life. I've heard that "You cannot judge a man by how much he has but by how much he is loved." If that is true, then my father was a truly blessed person, a man who was truly loved.

That night Daddy got worse. It was already Saturday night, and everyone was still in and out of the apartment since the previous Monday. He wasn't speaking at all anymore.

The next day I was in the bedroom with Dad. Mom was there too, and perhaps a few others. Suddenly Daddy began to stir, making some kind of movements with his hands. He had a smile on his face and he put his fingers to his lips as if he were trying to whistle, only no sound came out. Then he started making a "tying" movement, as though he were trying to tie a knot. We just stared and then suddenly Daddy "threw the rope" out. Mom realized what Daddy was doing.

"Look," she told me. "*Guarda*. He is back in *Castellamare* right now. He's on a boat, throwing the rope out into the water. Oh, my God.

Dio mio. Dio mio." I put an arm around Mom and kissed the side of her head as she wiped her eyes.

Later that day more people appeared at our house. Mom and us children were in the room with Dad, and Joe G. was sitting in a chair beside the bed. Suddenly Daddy opened his eyes and spoke again. He looked wildly at Joe, and his body almost convulsed as he grabbed his side. "Joe," he cried out. I was startled and Daddy noticed. Daddy turned to me and said, "No, Susie, no, *non ti preoccupare,"* telling me not to worry. He reached for my hand and looked at me. "Go in the kitchen, please, Baby, go inside. Daddy's okay."

He looked at Joe G. and softly said something in Sicilian. I couldn't hear or understand what it was. Mom was closer and understood. Daddy wanted the rest of us to leave so that Joe and Mom could change him. They were the only ones he'd let do that, and he didn't want the rest of us in the room when they did it. Joe G. did not leave the house those last days. There was nothing he would not do for Daddy. He helped Mom change Daddy and change the linens underneath him.

Mommy motioned for the rest of us to leave the room. I squeezed Daddy's hand, upset by his obvious pain. The medicine did not seem to be working anymore. He was grinding his teeth and his pale face was turning red now. Mom called out to Josephine, "Jo, call the doctor right away!"

Daddy looked at me and pulled on my hand. "It's okay, Baby, it's okay," he told me. "Go inside now."

I looked at my father and pouted like a little girl as tears came to my eyes. "I love you, *Papà,* I love you, Daddy!" as my voice cracked.

Daddy found the strength for a minute to caress my face and say, "I love you, Sweetheart." Those were the last words my father ever said to me. He looked at me in all his pain and smiled at his youngest daughter. I forced a smile through my tears. I think it was Ben who helped me off the bed but I can't be sure. Everything else is a little foggy now.

In no time at all, the doctor was running up the stairs. Mom unlocked the bedroom door and let him in. Then she locked it again. Then the door opened. "You have no choice, John, you have no choice. Your family is doing the best they can but they can't take care of you at home anymore. You need to be in the hospital!" He raised his voice to Dad, which he had never done before.

Suddenly commotion everywhere. Mommy was scrambling around grabbing stuff and sweating. I could hear Joe G. trying to make Daddy understand what the doctor was saying. The doctor himself had called the ambulance. Josephine came into the living room. "He's going to the hospital," she said. "He is having kidney failure. His whole stomach is all swollen." She was crying.

I heard the sirens blaring from the open windows. The doctor had sedated Daddy with an injection. He was unconscious now. I could not get through to my father in all the confusion once the ambulance arrived. Everyone was told to please stay out of the way.

As the EMT people carried Daddy downstairs on a stretcher, I pushed my way past everyone and ran to Daddy's bedroom window. I stuck my head out the window and saw my father's lifeless body on the stretcher as he was carried down the front steps. I saw some of the old ladies on the block making the sign of the cross when they realized it was Daddy. Some of them were kissing the crosses they wore on their necks. When the EMTs closed the door at the back of the ambulance and drove away, my body sank to the floor. I held my head in my hands and I cried. I cried, and I cried, and I cried.

I went to the hospital later on that day. I walked into a room where all I could hear was machines. I stared at my father on the bed. There were tubes all over him. I had to leave the room. I wanted to knock down every wall in that hospital, but instead I just paced up and down the corridor, unable to stay still. I wasn't sure if I was going to faint or throw up.

I went back in the room and looked at Daddy again and then I walked out of his room. Mom was sitting in a chair beside Daddy just staring at him and holding his hand. She held a rosary in the other hand and I could see her lips moving as she prayed.

Mom came into the corridor where I was then standing with my head against the wall. She gently put her hand on my arm and told me, "Go home. Don't worry. You don't have to stay here all night. I will stay with your father. He could be like this a long time."

"I'm not leaving," I said, and pulled away from my mother. I went back into Daddy's room. Now I stood beside his bed and held his hand. "I love you, *Papà*" I whispered to him, as tears rolled down my face. *Does he even hear me?* I wondered.

I bent down so that I could make Daddy's hand reach my face. I was caressing my cheek with Daddy's hand, trying to remember the way he smelled when I was a kid. He would lift me up in his arms and I would hug him so tight his face would turn red because he couldn't breathe. He would always laugh at how rough his little girl was. That's what I wanted to do right now. I wanted to rip out all those tubes and just give Daddy a great big hug. I wanted to kiss his face a million times. I wanted to scream, "Daddy, I love you! PLEASE wake up!" I wanted to hear my father's voice. Instead all I could hear were those damn machines. They were giving me a headache.

I had to leave as the night went on. Mom was going to spend the night, as she had so many nights before. I went home to an empty apartment and of course could not sleep. It was so quiet. Just that morning the house had been full. Now I was alone again. I started to clean up a little because we had all left in a hurry that afternoon. Then I just rocked back and forth in Daddy's chair until I fell asleep.

I had not been to work since Memorial Day. I had to go back the next day because I had used my vacation time. Some vacation. Mom and I needed the money. The doctor said Daddy could stay that way for days or even weeks. I would go back to the hospital after work on Monday.

***

The Last Day...June 4, 1990

Mom woke me up that morning with a phone call from the hospital. When I got to work my boss and my friends were all very supportive giving me hugs and words of encouragement. Nothing helped. I watched the clock all day. I kept calling the hospital to ask if there had been any change in Daddy's condition. NONE. With every moment that passed I remembered how I had spent the hours at Daddy's bedside the whole week before.

Each time I spoke with Mom she gave me an update on who had come in and out of Daddy's room that day. My sisters and brother had been there at different times throughout the day. Mom called me as I was getting ready to leave my job. *"Susie, perchè non vai in casa? No hai dormito niente per una settimana. Non c'è stato cambiamento con Papà. Puoi venire domani."* Mom was telling me to go straight home since I had not slept in a week. There was no change in my father's condition. She thought it best that I go the next day.

I told Mom I wasn't sure if I was going to come or not. I was not getting out of work until late. I wouldn't get to stay too long at the hospital at that hour anyway. I thought about it as I sat at my desk. *Should I go?* I got a nervous feeling in my gut. I thought about seeing Daddy the way I had the night before and tears came to my eyes. I remembered the noise in his room from the machines and that smell of alcohol throughout the hospital.

Then, in a moment of indecision, I made the biggest mistake of my life. I went straight home after work. I didn't go to the hospital on what turned out to be the last day of my father's life. It was an error in judgment I live with every single day. I went home to the apartment that night. Joey met me there. Together we sat quietly on the couch talking about my father and reminiscing about all the times Daddy made me go crazy with his rules and curfews. We laughed, thinking about the time I was sixteen and Daddy told me to use the light switch and the stereo in my room if I wanted to go dancing.

Joey brought up the time he and Dad got drunk while I was at work at the bakery. He told me how he and Daddy had cooked a whole pot of sauce that afternoon while they had the kitchen to themselves. "It was just us guys," he teased me. "That sauce was so good."

"I'm sure it tasted even better with a half a bottle of wine!" I said. We both laughed.

That day when I came home from work I was smiling to myself as I looked at Joey and Dad. They made such a big mess. I remember that cleaning the kitchen and living room took me at least two hours. Joey and Dad did not even hear me. When they finally woke up they found me sitting on the floor watching television. They started laughing as they noticed they had left all the cleaning up to me. They both told me, *"Thank you, grazie,"* when I teased them about how long it had taken me to clean up Joey and I were laughing.

I closed my eyes suddenly as I was about to cry. Joey pulled me into his arms and kissed my face. "I know, Baby. I know. Your father is a great man, Sue, a great man." I smiled through my tears and with a nod of my head I agreed with Joey.

Joey talked about his birthday and Dad's concern that Mom give him a gift despite his being in the hospital with pneumonia. Then Joey brought up Dad's birthday and how he would not take the picture with his sons-in-law until Joey got in the picture too. "That meant so much to me Sue, it really did."

"It meant a lot to me too," I said, caressing his cheek with my hand.

We sat quietly for a minute, not saying anything more. I lay my head on Joey's chest and was almost falling asleep. I sat up, suddenly agitated. Joey looked at me. "You okay, Sue?"

"No, I'm not okay, my father Joey, my father!" I cried. The phone rang.

Joey and I looked at each other and neither of us moved to answer it right away. It rang again and then I got up from the couch and went to answer it. My voice cracked as I answered the telephone, "He - llo." I said. Someone was clearing their throat. "He - llo."

"Susie," Mom said on the other end of the telephone line. "*Sei sola?*" she asked me, wanting to know if I was alone.

"No, *Mamma*, Joey is here with me. Josephine and Jack are next door with the kids," I told her. Joey saw me grip my chest and the color leave my face. He came to my side and listened. "*Mamma, che c'è, Papà, com'è Papà?*" I said, asking Mom what had happened, how was my father.

"*Papà non c'è più, Gioia, Papà non c'è più.*" Mom started to cry into the phone as she told me that my father "was no more." He was no longer with us.

"No, Mommy, no! Please! No!" I started to cry. Joey took the phone from my hand.

"I'm so sorry, Mom, I'm so sorry," he was telling my mother. Then "Yes, okay, yes, okay, Ma, okay. I won't leave her alone. Don't worry. Okay, Ma." He hung up the telephone and pulled me into his arms as I sobbed.

"My father, Joey, my father's gone! He's gone, Oh, my God! He's gone!" I was crying.

Joey and I heard the telephone ringing next door through the kitchen wall. Then within less than five minutes someone was knocking at the door. I sat down in Dad's chair as Joey went to answer the door. It was Josephine with red, puffy eyes. When Joey answered the door Josephine started to cry. Joey hugged her tightly and she sobbed on his shoulder. "I'm sorry Jo, I'm so sorry," he told my sister.

My sister walked toward me and I stood up. We embraced and our shoulders were rising and falling at the same time as we cried together. "He's gone, Baby. Daddy's gone." I didn't answer. We let go of each other and straightened up. We wiped our eyes and took a deep breath. *The hospital, Mom, I have to go there, now,* I thought. Josephine spoke again. "We have to go, Sue. We have to get to the hospital before they take Daddy a - way." Her voice cracked.

"I know, I know," I agreed. "Let's go, Jo, let's go."

"Jack called a cab already. We have to go. Jack's going to stay with the kids." Josephine told me.

Just as we had the day of Daddy's first surgery, Josephine and I held hands in the cab all the way to the hospital. We didn't even speak to each other. We sat there quietly, each of us constantly sniffling and wiping tears from our faces.

We got out in front of the hospital and went right up. The security guards already knew our family and knew Daddy. Word had already spread to the employees that one of their former co-workers had died right there in their hospital. "I'm sorry, ladies" one of the guards said. "We will all miss John. He was a great guy" he told us.

"Thank you, thank you." Josephine and I answered together.

We went up on the elevator and when we stepped off, the first face that I saw was Zia Adriana's. Her eyes were red and swollen. She was wearing a grey T-shirt and black leggings. I don't know why I remember that, but somehow I do. Maybe the sadness of the colors matched my state of mind.

She opened up her arms to me and I went right into them. "*Zia,*" I cried, "*Zia, Papà non c' è più!*" NO MORE. Suddenly I heard my mother's voice. She was sitting in a chair, and I hadn't seen her behind the other family members standing in front of her. Word had spread fast.

As soon as she saw me, Mom started to scream and hold her head with her hands as if she wanted to pull her hair out. *"È colpa mia!"* she yelled out, *"È colpa mia!"* screaming that it was her fault. I looked at her confused. What could possibly be her fault? She had not left Daddy's side until he took his last breath. I went over to my mother.

"Mamma," I said, as I smoothed her hair and hugged her. She pushed me away to look at my face.

"I'm sorry, *Gioia mia,* I'm sorry!" Mom said to me. Then she put her arms around me and was sobbing. I held on to her and rubbed her back.

I was on my knees in front of my mother and she kept apologizing to me through her tears. "No, Mommy," I told her. *It was not her fault my father died. It was not her fault. Why was she apologizing to me?*

Then it made sense. Mom blamed herself for my not going to the hospital that night, she told me, crying, *"È colpa mia.* I told you to go home. You were so tired. You didn't sleep all week. You were so upset yesterday. I told you to go home to rest. *È colpa mia!* It's my fault. Your father," she said. "Your father looked for you. He opened his eyes. *"'SUSIE!,'* ha chiamato, *'SUSIE!' Puoi s'è chiuso l'occhi per sempre. L'ultima parola della bocca sua è stata 'SUSIE!'"*

I almost fainted. I let go of Mom and lay my head on the chair beside her. I could barely hear anything. *Oh, my God. Oh, my God. Mom told me Daddy opened his eyes and looked for me. He called out my name. "Susie," Daddy called out. He called out for me. My name was the last word he ever said. "Susie," he called. BUT I WASN'T THERE! Oh, my God, please forgive me. Daddy, please forgive me. I WASN'T THERE!*

My brother Benny came over and lifted me up by my arms. I could not look at him in the eye. He hugged me. He held me tight and rubbed my back. "It's okay, Baby," he said in my ear. "It's okay. Come on, Baby. Come and say goodbye now. They have to take Daddy away. Come and say goodbye," he told me.

Ben walked with me into Daddy's room. I went to Daddy's side and Ben stayed at the foot of the bed, allowing me a minute to be with my father. I looked down at my father. No more tubes. No more noise. Daddy's hair looked like it had grown in. He had salt and pepper peach fuzz on his head. I smiled.

I bent down and kissed his face. He was still warm. I kissed his cheek again. I lifted his hand, I caressed my cheek with his fingertips. I whispered in his ear, "I'm sorry, *Papà*, I'm sorry. I love you so much, Daddy. I love you so much." I put my cheek next to his and held onto his hand. "I love you Daddy, I love you." I kept saying it. My brother walked out of the room.

I heard Benny tell Joe G., "Joe, please go get my sister. She's breaking my heart."

Suddenly Joe G. was beside me. "Come on, Susie, come on. We have to leave because they have to take Daddy downstairs. They waited for us but they have to take him now. Come on." Joe took my hand from Daddy's and he squeezed it. He kissed me gently on my cheek. "Come on, Sue" he told me again, "We have to leave now." He let me give Daddy one more kiss on his face.

And I whispered again in his ear, "I love you, Daddy, I love you." I walked into the corridor as people with white coats and plastic gloves were walking toward Daddy's room to take his body away. I walked quickly back into the waiting room where Mom and the others were.

Zia Adriana came to me once more and hugged me again. I held on to her tightly. When I pulled away from Zia her grey shirt was drenched with my sweat and my tears. My hair was all wet. I felt faint and had to sit down.

I have no idea how I got back home from the hospital. I can't remember. I only remember Mom sitting in one of the dining room chairs and I stood beside her with my arms around her shoulders. She was not crying anymore and neither was I. We were just quietly comforting one another. She had her arms around me too, and laid her head on my chest.

Joe G. sat in a chair across from Mom. He was asking her questions and giving her information about the funeral arrangements he had made. Daddy would be laid out at the funeral parlor whose owners had the same last name as ours. I think they came from Sicily too, but there was no relation. Many of the Italians in the neighborhood trusted them with their loved ones.

Mom just nodded her head at Joe's questions, approving and appreciating everything Joe G. had done for Daddy. *"Grazie,"* she told Joe. *"Grazie, figio mio. Grazie."* She thanked Joe as she patted his hand.

I could not stand on my feet anymore. I felt weak. I went to sit beside my Joey on the couch. Mom had gone into her bedroom to change her clothes. Joey put his arms around me and I laid my head back so that our faces were cheek to cheek. He turned and kissed my cheek. "I'm sorry, Baby" he whispered in my ear. "I loved your father, Sue. He was a really good man." I closed my eyes and was grateful to be in Joey's arms. I held onto his hands as he squeezed me closer. *What happens now?* I thought. *What the hell happens now?*

I opened my eyes and looked up at Fran's wedding photographs hanging above the couch in the living room. We were all smiling. So happy to be in that photograph. Mom and Daddy were sitting for the group picture. They sat in two chairs beside each other holding hands, their children standing together beside them. *My family*, I thought, *my family*. I looked at each of my siblings around the room that night. The night our father left us.

Maria and Fran were walking around, nervously cleaning up as usual. They were taking glasses and napkins off the dining room table while people were not even finished drinking yet. Maria was biting her lip. Fran's shoulders were rising up and down from hiccups after she had cried earlier.

Josephine was in the kitchen near the open window. She was

drinking espresso and smoking a cigarette. She was not crying. Now she was pissed off. She was so angry. She was cursing under her breath. She was almost ranting. "This can't be, this can't be!" she was saying. Jack was behind her, rubbing her shoulders.

My little nephews had lost their two grandfathers within three months. Two men who loved them so much. Two men whom they adored since they were babies. I felt so bad for them. They were trying to be brave, or perhaps they were too scared of what was going on around them. They were just sitting around the living room, not making noise, not playing. They had been awakened from their sleep when they heard their mother cry. They did not want to stay in their beds. They wanted to be with Nonna, they told Josephine.

Mom hugged them tightly as she held them close to her. All three of them in one tight embrace when she saw them come into our apartment. "Nonno loved you so much. You never forget that," she told them. They held back their tears. Then they walked to different corners of the room to cry without being noticed. I noticed anyway as I watched them.

I had taken Johnnie from Jack's arms. "Please let me hold him. I need my godson right now." Jack smiled at me as he handed his son over to me. He kissed my forehead as he squeezed my arm without saying a word. He winked at me with his red eyes. I squeezed his hand, knowing exactly how my brother-in-law had felt only three months earlier when he lost his own father. Now he had lost Daddy, too. My brother Ben was sitting in Daddy's chair, just staring into space and biting his nails. He was not speaking to anyone. Ben's wife was home with Christina. She was already seven months pregnant with their next baby.

Now we'd have the next part to get through, Daddy's farewell. I was not looking forward to it. In the days that followed we had services for Dad. Two days of a wake at the funeral parlor. Then on the third day the funeral mass and the burial at the cemetery. The mass would be at the parish where I attended Catholic school. In the same church where Daddy beamed as my name was called several times at the eighth grade graduation ceremony.

Fran kept pointing out my name in the program. "*Guarda, Papà,*" she would say, showing him my name on the page. "First honors," she told him, which meant I had a straight A average on my report card and had made Principal's List. Daddy looked at me and smiled, pointing to my name in the program as he winked at me. I smiled at him. *Daddy was proud of me,* I remember thinking.

At the wake the funeral director had to open up a second room because there were so many flowers, they lined the entire room. There were so many people too. Our family, with all the aunts, uncles, and cousins, was already too much for one room. Then there were so many friends. People waited in line to pay their respects to Daddy.

The last night at the funeral home the priest came by afterwards to give his blessing. I went out to the parking lot, touched by the priest's words and so, so, sad, that my father was really gone. As people started to leave, my godparents found me with Joey in the parking lot.

Zio Achille tapped Joey on the shoulder and asked him to please let go of me so he could speak to his godchild. Joey stepped aside as he patted Zio Achille on the back. My godfather and I embraced. "*Zio, mio padre mi ha lasciato. Zio, mio padre non c'è più.*" I cried on his shoulder telling my godfather that my father had *left me.* Zio Achille kissed my cheek.

My godmother, Zia Maria, stood behind me smoothing back my hair and rubbing my back, just as she had when my grandfather died almost a decade before. She was still calling me her baby. "I'm sorry, Baby *mia,*" she said through her own tears. "I'm so sorry."

Zio Achille pulled away to look at me. With his own hand he wiped the tears from my face. "*Senti, figiozza mia,*" he said, telling me in Sicilian to listen to what he was about to tell me. "I know I am not your father. Nobody could take your father's place, NEVER." he told me. "But I am your godfather and I love you so much. If you need me I am always here for you. Anything you need. *Mi capisci, bambina mia?*' Did I understand his promise? I tried to smile at him and he patted my face with his hand then once more he kissed my cheek. I held onto my godfather and held my godmother's hand at my side. I loved them so much.

Zio Achille kept his word and in the next several years he and I grew even closer than ever. He and Zia Maria separated again, so he lived by himself in an apartment close by to my house. He would cook me dinner on some Sundays and we would always get together for our birthdays and the holidays, even if it wasn't on the same day of the holiday. We would have a birthday dinner and then a Christmas dinner as well. One year I bought him a gold charm that read, *#1 Godfather* and he was so honored. Five months later for my birthday he had Frankie and Doreen, his son and daughter-in-law, pick out a chain and a charm for me that read *#1 Godchild*. When Zio Achille moved to Florida to be reunited with Zia Maria, I would wear that necklace with the little charm, touching it often to think about my godfather and how he had been there for me when my father died. I was so grateful.

I always did listen to my godfather and the advice he would offer when I needed it most. His theme song was Frank Sinatra's "My Way." If there was one thing my godfather taught me, it was to have no regrets. And although I usually agreed with him, for one mistake in my life, I cannot.

My regret is not seeing my father on the last day of his life. I will tell you something I have never told anyone, not my mother, not even my husband. It was not because of my mother that I didn't go to the hospital that day. Not because I was tired. I did not go to the hospital on purpose. On the last day of my father's life, as naïve as I was, I thought Daddy would wait for me. As selfish as I was, I thought he would not let go until he saw my face once more. I thought if I just waited *one day*, it would be one more day my father would be on this earth with all of us.

For at least a year after Daddy's death, every time Mom told the story of Daddy's last breath, or his last words, I cringed. I would have to leave the room. I heard the story a million times. She just kept telling it because she felt so guilty. *"È colpa mia"* is how she would end the story each time. But I knew it was not her fault. It was my own.

That first year after Daddy's death I slept beside my mother in her bed every night. I had to keep my hand on her shoulder each night as she slept. My hand would rise up and down as she breathed. For months I had nightmares. I would dream of an open coffin…each time I got close to the coffin there were only bones inside. Sometimes I dreamed about Memorial Day when I carried Daddy to his bed, except that in my nightmares Daddy's body would turn to dust as I was walking. I would fall to my knees, trying to put the dust together and screaming in my sleep. Mom would wake me. "It's okay, *Gioia, stai sognare, stai sognare!*" Dreaming. Nightmares. Only Nightmares.

* * *

A Temporary Conclusion

The rest of the family took Daddy's death as badly as Mom and I had. Things changed that year and would always be different. Mom cries every Valentine's Day, remembering our chocolate breakfasts. Joe G. and Maria are still living in Queens, where they now host an occasional Sunday dinner. We spend Christmas Eves at their house too. Josephine, Ben, and Francesca have all gone through divorces. Josephine's boys are now men. They have all brought girlfriends into the family whom we all consider nieces already. Benny has three daughters, Christina, Michelle, and Amanda. Three strong young women who can hold their own with their father, just what Benny needed. Although Ben and Josephine have since moved to Long Island, Francesca was the only one of us who left New York. She was tired of the cold winters and congested streets. Now she lives in the Southwest with her two daughters, Francesca and Silvana. It's difficult being away from them.

In case you were wondering, I married my Joey. We were blessed with an amazing child, a bright little boy who keeps us on our toes. He is named for his paternal grandfather and we call him Tony. My Tony. My Joey. My boys.

Our family has been through so much since Daddy's death. Each one of us dealing with our own issues: failed marriages, depression, financial hardships. And for me - *two* miscarriages. One thing we do all have in common is that we are survivors. Thanks to our parents. Thanks to our childhood. The best thing my parents ever gave me, that my family ever gave me, was LOVE. So much love. So much that it fills my heart. So much that I could share it with others. Especially with my own family, my husband, and my son.

I hope you have enjoyed my story, which has taken a lot of heart and so much strength to write. Our story continues. Everyone's life changing every year, every day, every moment.

For all the Italian Americans who read this, as I said to my son the day Italy won the World Cup in the summer of 2006: **Be proud, be very proud!**

Our parents and grandparents have given us many gifts. The gift of family. The gift of pride. The gift of great food. Great wine. Great friends. Great stories, like this one. A great story….**An Italian American Story**.